THE WEST POINT STORY

Like the United States itself, the United States Military Academy had a difficult time coming of age. Nearly abolished by Congress several times, its famous traditions were finally established when Sylvanus Thayer was given command of the academy.

This is the story of West Point, from its early struggle for survival to its position today as an important source of leadership for America in peace and war.

THE
WEST POINT
STORY

by COLONEL RED REEDER

and NARDI REEDER CAMPION

Illustrated with

U.S. Army photographs

RANDOM HOUSE · NEW YORK

ACKNOWLEDGMENTS

We wish to acknowledge our debt to the authors whose works have been invaluable to us in writing this Landmark book. We referred to the works of many, many authors. The principal ones were: Sidney Forman, *West Point;* Ernest Dupuy, *Where They Have Trod;* Edward C. Boynton, *History of West Point;* John Crane and James F. Kieley, *West Point, Key to America;* Carl Van Doren, *Secret History of the American Revolution;* Marquis James, *They Had Their Hour;* Francis T. Miller, *General Douglas MacArthur* and *Eisenhower, Man and Soldier;* Clark Lee and Richard Henschel, *Douglas MacArthur;* Alden Hatch, *General Ike, A Biography of Dwight David Eisenhower;* Edward S. Wallace, *The Great Reconnaissance* and *General William Jenkins Worth;* A. L. Conger, *The Rise of U. S. Grant;* Douglas Southall Freeman, *R. E. Lee;* P. R. Moody, *Leaders of the War Between the States;* Morris Schaff, *The Spirit of Old West Point;* Joseph P. Farley, *West Point in the Early Sixties;* Tim Cohane, *The Gridiron Grenadiers;* Alexander M. Weyand, *Saga of American Football;* Robert L. Eichelberger, *Our Jungle Road to Tokyo.*

We also benefited by the use of old records and scrapbooks at the United States Military Academy Library and at the United States Military Academy Museum.

We thank Colonel William J. Morton, a distinguished graduate of West Point and the Academy's librarian, for his helpful guidance.

RED REEDER

NARDI REEDER CAMPION

To
Thomas Baird Campion
with admiration unlimited

CONTENTS

THE WEST POINT STORY

/

Washington Hall is large enough to seat 2,700 cadets at one time.

WEST POINT

On a warm July day last year, seven hundred new cadets marched in formation down Jefferson Road at West Point, the glint of the sun's rays flashing on the visors of their caps.

To the left of the tremendous mess hall stood nine Explorer Scouts. The Explorers watched the companies change from "platoon front" into a "column of squads" and sweep up the steps into

Washington Hall. Snare drums and fifes sounded blood-tingling music and then the bugles blared in.

As the last company of cadets entered the building, a fat scout with carrot-colored hair ran up the mess hall steps. His nose twitched as he inhaled the odors of roast beef and pastry which floated through the screen doors.

The Explorer Scout Advisor, standing in the center of the group of scouts, called, "Hey, Stubby Butterfield! You better come back. You don't belong up there. Besides, you've had enough to eat."

The red-headed scout did not hear his leader. The boy was fascinated by what he saw.

Each cadet was standing silently before his place in the mess hall. The white tablecloths sparkled with shining silverware and clean dishes. Overhead hung the flags of every state in the Union. A voice commanded, "Take seats!" and the silence was broken by the scraping of countless chairs and by the chatter of the cadets.

Waiters in white coats pushed through the kitchen doors carrying stainless-steel pitchers. Stubby Butterfield heard a waiter say to a plebe (a new cadet) at a table near the door, "Mister, if you want any more iced tea, let me know."

Suddenly a cadet dressed in white trousers and a close fitting gray coat opened the screen doors and looked out at Stubby. On the cadet's upper sleeve were the four stripes of a cadet captain.

"Sorry," he said apologetically, "I have to ask you to wait until the mess hall is open to visitors. They'll let you in after the meal is over and the tables have been cleared."

The Explorer grinned. "All right. You're not one of the plebes, are you?"

"No. I'm a firstie. First classman, that is."

Stubby retreated with dignity and joined the Explorers who were strolling past Central Barracks toward the clock tower. The Advisor approached an M.P. on duty at the road intersection.

"Can you tell us what to see here that's of interest?" the Advisor asked. "We have two hours to spend."

The Military Policeman lifted his hand to caution the driver of an automobile and the car slowed down. Then the M.P. shoved his thumbs behind the buckle of his pistol belt and regarded the visitor with interest.

"Why don't you go down to that big stone building?" he suggested. "It's the museum. The Military Academy museum's got everything from Indian tomahawks and General Pershing's war map down to that Nazi General Goering's baton. That stick's got a million dollars' worth of jewels on it. Or you can go over to the library. It's got more'n just books. I went in there myself yesterday to show a friend the paintin' of General Lee. It's hangin' 'longside of the picture of the West Pointer that beat him. General Grant."

The Advisor turned to his troop.

"Well, shall we start with the museum or the library?"

The fat redhead spoke to a tall boy at his side.

"Hey, Jimmy. Let's me and you go back to the mess hall and watch the plebes come out."

The Advisor looked at the big clock on the ivy-covered tower of the West Academic Building.

"All right. It's ten minutes to one. We'll meet here in two hours."

Stubby Butterfield and Jimmy Smith walked

back along the street in front of Central Barracks. It was pleasant in the shade of the elms. To the right stretched the wide Plain, or parade ground, its close clipped grass shamrock-green in the sun. Across the road were football fields, tennis courts, a baseball diamond and a soccer field. The natural beauty was impressive. Beyond the Plain towered Storm King Mountain. The Hudson River, a ribbon of blue-gray, swept around West Point and flowed on to New York City, forty miles to the south. On a hill in back of the great gray mess hall rose the Cadet Chapel, as if standing guard over the Academy.

"I had no idea West Point was so large," said Stubby.

Jimmy Smith did not answer. He was studying a bronze statue just ahead. It was of a young man in uniform holding a sword high overhead; his left arm gripped a bronze flag; the muzzle of a cannon jutted out behind the figure. The boys read the inscription on the marble pedestal stating that the monument had been presented to West Point by the cadets of the French Military Academy, *L'Ecole Polytechnique.* The monument repre-

Cadet Chapel seen from across the Plain

sented the spirit of the French cadets fighting for their country.

The two friends walked toward another statue near by and read the inscription carved on its gray stone base:

COLONEL THAYER
FATHER OF THE MILITARY ACADEMY

Stubby Butterfield held up his hand.

"Listen!"

From the mess hall came the bark of a loudspeaker: "THE FIRST PERIOD OF AFTERNOON SCHEDULE IS CHANGED AS FOLLOWS. FIRST AND SECOND COMPANIES WILL ATTEND INSTRUCTION IN TENT PITCHING AND DISPLAY OF EQUIPMENT. THIRD AND FOURTH COMPANIES WILL MARCH TO THE CADET STORE TO TRY ON FULL-DRESS COATS. FIFTH AND SIXTH COMPANIES WILL REPORT TO THE ELECTRICITY LECTURE ROOM TO SEE THE TRAINING FILM ON DRIVER INSTRUCTION. REST! TAKE CHARGE OF YOUR COMPANIES!"

The mess hall doors opened and out poured a stream of plebes in light gray trousers and steel-blue shirts. With them was a sprinkling of first classmen dressed in gray dress coats, white trousers and white cotton gloves. The plebes were double-timing toward their barracks; the firsties were walking. The difference in gait as well as the difference in uniforms made it easy to distinguish the two classes.

The cadet who had spoken to Stubby on the steps of the mess hall stopped and said, "I'm sorry I couldn't invite you Scouts in."

"We have already eaten, anyhow," said Jimmy Smith. "Thanks."

"Where is your troop from?" the cadet wanted to know. "I was an Explorer Scout once. Troop Two, Long Prairie, Minnesota."

"We're from Baltimore," Stubby put in. "We're going up to Canada to a jamboree. The rest of our gang is down at the museum."

"My roommate's from Maryland," observed the cadet. "Hagerstown. My other roommate lived in Baltimore, but he hails from Arkansas, from such a small town it's not even on the map." The cadet grinned in a friendly manner.

Stubby fingered the blue ribbon of his God and Country Award which hung above his heart. He glanced at the statue of Colonel Thayer, then at the firstie.

"I'd like to become a cadet," he said, "but I'm no genius."

The first classman grinned again.

"If you graduate from a high school and are average in your studies, and apply yourself, you can do all right here," he told Stubby. "But you have to be between seventeen and twenty-two and you have to pass physical and mental exams to get in."

Jimmy Smith said, "Is that all you have to do to be a cadet? How much does it cost?"

"It doesn't cost anything. The government pays you a hundred and eleven dollars a month to come here. You buy your uniforms and textbooks out of that. But first you have to get an appointment. My congressman appointed me. One of my roommates got his appointment through the National Guard. The other won his at an Honor military school."

"How about your food?" asked Stubby, licking his lips. "How many cadets are there, and can they all eat at once?"

"Stubby always asks about food," explained Jimmy. "He managed to eat most of the way up from Maryland."

The cadet laughed.

"Each cadet—there are twenty-four hundred in the Corps—receives money to cover the cost of his food. They can feed all of us a hot meal at one sitting, and the food's good, Stubby."

"You come here for four years, don't you?" asked Jimmy.

"Right. When I graduate next June I'll get a degree in engineering and be commissioned as a second lieutenant. I expect to go in the Armor. That's tanks."

"What time do the plebes have to get up in the morning?" asked Stubby.

"Five-fifty. Not only the plebes—all the rest of us, too. The reveille gun fires at the same time summer or winter."

Stubby made a face.

"Brother! That's awful early."

The graduating class receives the final salute of the Corps at Graduation Parade.

Immediately after Graduation Parade the upper classmen "recognize" the plebes in the Central Area of cadet barracks.

"Oh, it isn't too bad. After reveille we have fifteen minutes to put our rooms in order and make
our beds. Then we march to breakfast. We have
classes all morning during the school year. Dinner
at noon. After that, classes until three-fifteen. We
all look forward to the athletic period which be-
gins right after class. If you're not on a varsity
squad you go to company sports twice a week.
Some fellows belong to clubs like the Radio Club,
the Model Railway Club, the Glee Club, the
Camera Club, the Debate Club and so on. There's
lots to do here. After supper you go to your room
and study till taps. Taps blows at ten."

"Do you like it?" asked Jimmy.

"I certainly do, or I wouldn't be here."

"Did you like it when you were a plebe?" per-
sisted Jimmy. "I hear plebe summer is a rugged
deal."

The firstie pulled a white handkerchief from
the sleeve of his dress coat and mopped the sweat
band of his gray cap. Then he put the cap back on
his head and centered the black visor over his
nose.

"The plebe year is hard, but it isn't something

you can't take." The cadet grinned. "I stood it. Thousands of others have, too. It's like earning your spurs was in medieval times. Being a first classman isn't any cinch, either. We have to break in all these plebes."

Stubby Butterfield cleared his throat.

"If you have such a full day with studies and all, when do you receive your military training?"

"In the summertime. The yearlings and second classmen are away from West Point right now taking special military instruction. You fellows'll have to excuse me. I hope you have a good time at your jamboree."

Stubby glanced at the folder in his hand.

"They gave this to me when we came through the gate." He read aloud the words at the top of the pamphlet: "Duty, Honor, Country."

The firstie had turned away but now he stopped and faced the boys.

"That's our motto," he said. "It's very important to each one of us."

"What do you mean?" asked Stubby.

"This morning, when I was explaining that motto to the plebes, I asked one of them to tell in

A cadet reciting in Military
History class

Cadet sailing club at Lake Popolopen, Camp Buckner, near West
Point.

his own words what the motto meant to him. He had a fine answer. He said, 'About *Duty*. That comes above your family or yourself. *Honor*. Is a thing right or wrong? *Country*. I mean to defend it. I'll fight for it.' "

The crisp notes of a bugle sounded across the Plain. The plebe class ran out of barracks, formed ranks in the street, and marched off for afternoon instruction. The firstie snapped to attention and saluted as a two-star general walked by. The general returned the salute, nodded at the two scouts, and walked on.

"That's the Superintendent," volunteered the firstie softly. "He's the highest ranking officer on the post. Once he was a cadet himself. Played on the football team."

"About your motto," said Stubby after a pause. "The first part of the Boy Scout oath is something like the West Point motto. Ours starts, 'On my honor, I will do my best to do my duty to God and my Country, and to obey the Scout Law.' "

"Right," replied the cadet. "More'n half of the Corps were Boy Scouts. The ideals are much the same." A note of pride entered his voice. "West

Point is a hard place. I hope it always remains that way." The cadet looked up at the statue of Colonel Thayer. "It had a rugged beginning."

Stubby Butterfield glanced at his wrist watch.

"We have a little over an hour. Where do you recommend we start to learn about West Point?"

"I suggest you walk over to Trophy Point. You'll find memorials and trophies there from the Korean War all the way back to the Great Chain."

"The Great Chain?" repeated Stubby Butterfield. "What's that?"

The West Pointer laughed. "Read up on your history and find out," he said. "You'll be surprised how many exciting things happened around here during the American Revolution—not to mention the years following that. The West Point story is linked closely to the story of our country."

View of the Hudson River, looking north from Trophy Point

THE GREAT CHAIN

More than three hundred years ago, Henry Hudson sailed his ship *The Half Moon* up the broad river that was to bear his name. When he reached the first sharp bend, he dropped anchor. The point of land nearest him later became known as West Point.

This particular spot was very important in the Revolutionary War. George Washington called

19

West Point "the key to America." There were no railroads or paved highways in those days, so rivers were of first importance. The control of the Hudson River was one of the main issues fought out in the Revolution. Whichever force held this strong point above the river controlled a water-course which could be used to separate the New England states from the rest of the country.

In the early days many forts and blockhouses were built to protect West Point. Count Thaddeus Kosciusko, the great Polish patriot who was helping the colonists fight the British, planned and directed the fortifications. Today at West Point you can still see his work in Fort Putnam and Fort Clinton, and in the West Point Museum is Kosciusko's sword, engraved: "Draw me not without reason; sheath me not without honor." Fort Clinton was originally named Fort Arnold in honor of General Benedict Arnold, "the hero of Quebec." After Arnold betrayed his country the name was changed.

Many strange things took place at West Point during the Revolution. For one thing, an adventurous girl from Plymouth, Massachusetts, named

Kosciusko's Monument at West Point

Deborah Simpson, dressed herself as a man and enlisted in the regiment stationed on the post. She served in the army for a year before anyone found out she was a girl!

But nothing in American history is stranger than the story of the Great Chain.

The Americans wanted to be sure no enemy ships got up the Hudson. They decided to make a giant iron chain and stretch it across the river at the narrowest place. This was a big job. The chain had to be 1,700 feet long. It was forged at the Sterling Iron Works near West Point and when it was finished it weighed 150 tons and cost about $2,000 per ton.

Getting this heavy chain across the river was a tremendous feat. It was mounted on logs and floated across. The ends were bolted into rocks on the shore and fastened by huge blocks of wood and stone.

Once the chain was in place it was kept from sinking by logs and held fast by many anchors. In front of it was a "boom," made of logs lashed together, which was supposed to take the first shock of an approaching ship. A number of batteries were built on shore, their cannons pointed so as to guard the valuable chain.

Each winter the Hudson River was frozen solid, so the chain had to be taken up in the fall—another big job. It was coiled in a huge pile on the river bank until spring, when the patriots put it back in place.

After the Revolutionary War, the chain was taken apart and sold for scrap. A few remaining links are on display at Trophy Point overlooking the Hudson.

Cadets learn in the study of tactics that a defense which is never tested by the enemy may still serve its purpose. The Great Chain, with its guardian forts, was such an obstacle. The British men-of-war never dared test the Great Chain and the embattled colonists kept control of the all-important Hudson River.

The figurine of a cadet in Revolutionary uniform. The picture was taken looking north up the Hudson River from West Point.

THE MAN WHO TRIED
TO SELL WEST POINT

On the walls of the Old Cadet Chapel, in the West Point cemetery, are black marble shields bearing the names of the American generals who fought against the British in the Revolutionary War. From one shield the name has been erased, leaving only this inscription:

24

MAJOR GENERAL
Born 1740

The man whose name was scraped off was one of the bravest and most daring officers in American history—and one of the most dishonest. *He was a traitor.*

His name was Benedict Arnold.

Arnold grew up in a strict New England family. When he was fourteen he ran away from home to fight in the French and Indian Wars. As soon as he tired of fighting, he deserted. Thus Benedict Arnold began his disastrous military career as a deserter.

Arnold was a handsome man. He had black hair, dark skin, and very light eyes. He was strong and heavy-set but moved quickly. He had three weaknesses: a hot temper, an inability to handle money, and a habit of not telling the truth.

During the Revolution, Arnold became a brigadier general in the American Army. He fought under Ethan Allen of Vermont at Ticonderoga. He did a good job until he began to argue with Gen-

eral Allen over who was in command. Later
he led American forces in an attempt to capture Quebec. His daring work on the battlefield
brought him two wounds and he became a public
hero.

Then Arnold married Peggy Shippen, the
daughter of a Tory. She was the darling of Philadelphia society. The Arnolds lived on a more lav-
ish scale than they could afford, and soon they
were deep in debt.

His need of money was one reason why Arnold
became a traitor. There were other reasons as
well. He was angry because others were promoted before he was. He was angry because he
was accused of misusing government funds in
Pennsylvania. And he listened to bad advice.
Many of his wife's friends told him the colonies
would be better off if they remained with England.

So Benedict Arnold decided in cold blood to do
business with the enemy.

First he persuaded General Washington to
send him to West Point. Then he wrote the British
(and his letters have been preserved to this day):

"I have accepted the command at West Point as a post in which I can render the most essential services."

Already he was plotting his terrible deed.

After General Arnold saw West Point for the first time he wrote the British: "It is surprising a post of so much importance should be so neglected. . . . I am convinced the boom or chain thrown across the river to stop the shipping cannot be depended on. A single ship, large and heavy loaded, with a strong wind and tide, would break the chain."

Benedict Arnold went about the business of treason craftily. Five days after taking over the command of West Point he wrote General Washington and asked for a map of the country between West Point and New York "which would be very useful to me."

Then he wrote a *code* letter to the British in New York: "If I point out a plan . . . by which Sir Henry shall possess himself of West Point . . . £20,000 sterling I think will be a cheap purchase for an object of so much importance . . . A personal interview with an officer that you can confide in is absolutely necessary to plan matters."

Arnold waited anxiously for an answer. He was a man of action who had to act or else be sick. He could not stand delay.

Sir Henry Clinton, the British commander, sent word that his Adjutant General, Major John André, would meet secretly with Benedict Arnold to discuss terms.

Major André sailed up the Hudson on the British sloop *Vulture*, under a flag of truce, and anchored at Croton Point. About midnight he was rowed ashore by two farmers who, under General Arnold's orders, had muffled the oars in sheepskins so as to make no noise.

André sat silent in the stern while he traveled two miles across the broad Hudson. He was wearing a dark blue cape over his scarlet uniform. We can imagine that this brave British officer disliked meeting a traitor stealthily at night—but his duty was to obey orders.

General Arnold and Major André met on the river bank about two miles below Haverstraw. It was a moonless night and they "hid among the firs." From what we know of Benedict Arnold, it is safe to guess that the first thing they talked about was money. Once that was settled, they could work out a plan for the surrender of West Point.

General Arnold outlined a plot that must have taken Major André's breath away.

Arnold planned to turn over to the British not only the important highland forts, but also General George Washington himself!

Washington was coming to West Point soon and Benedict Arnold meant to arrange things so that in the confusion of the action the Commander-in-Chief and his entire staff would be captured by the enemy.

The secret meeting lasted until 4 A.M. Then Arnold came down the bank and tried to persuade the farmers to row Major André back to the *Vulture*. It was almost daylight and the farmers refused. They said they were too tired and sleepy.

Sometimes the course of history is changed by little things. If these men had rowed André back that night, perhaps the traitorous plot would never have been discovered and West Point and

George Washington would have fallen into the hands of the enemy.

As it was, Major André hid in General Arnold's quarters to wait until the next night to return to his ship. This was in direct violation of Sir Henry Clinton's order: "Do not go within an enemy's post."

Meanwhile, the Americans fired on the *Vulture*. The cannonade lasted for an hour, and the British ship was driven downstream, leaving André high and dry. General Arnold told André he would have to travel by horseback down the river to meet the British. Major André objected, but Arnold insisted.

Then Benedict Arnold tried to persuade André to change his uniform for civilian clothes. At first Major André did not want to, because once out of uniform his status would be that of a spy. And a spy, if captured by the enemy, could expect only one form of punishment—death.

Finally, Major André agreed. He took off his scarlet British coat and put on a purple one with gold buttons. Over it he put the blue cloak he had worn ashore.

General Arnold wrote a "pass" which said:

> Permit Mr. John Anderson to pass to White
> Plains, or below, if he chooses; he being on
> public business by my direction.
>
> B. ARNOLD

"Mr. John Anderson" carried papers in Benedict Arnold's handwriting which described the West Point fortifications and plans of defense. (André explained later at his trial, "Arnold made me put the papers I bore between my stocking and my feet.")

General Arnold said, "In case of any accident these papers *must* be destroyed."

At dusk André and Joshua Smith, the guide Arnold had gotten for him, set out on horseback. They ferried across the river and landed at Peekskill. After riding two hours they were challenged by an American sentry.

"Where are you going?"

"To Major Strang's," was the reply.

"Major Strang is not home," the sentry said.

"Then," said Joshua Smith, "we'll go to my old friend Colonel Drake's."

"Drake has moved away. Let me see your pass."

The sentry examined the pass carefully, then said, "Proceed."

Near Cat Hill Joshua Smith turned back, leaving Major André to ride alone the fifteen miles to the British in White Plains. At a bridge above Tarrytown, Major André was halted by three Westchester patriots: John Paulding, David Williams and Isaac Van Wart.

"Gentlemen," said André, "I hope you belong to our party."

"What party is that?"

"The lower party," said André, meaning the British down the river.

The patriots said they did. André was relieved. For some unknown reason he blurted out, "I am a British officer."

"We are Americans," said the patriots, "and you are our prisoner."

André tried then to say that he, too, was an American. He showed General Arnold's pass, but it was too late. The men ordered him to dismount. They searched him and found the papers in his shoes. The only man who could read pored over the papers for a long time. Finally he announced, "He's a spy!"

Major André tried frantically to buy the men off. He offered them his horse, saddle, and ten thousand guineas. But the three Americans were not for sale. They marched their prisoner to the nearest American post.

Major André argued with the American colonel. "If you will send word of my arrest to General Arnold, you will find out you have made a mistake."

The colonel sent this message to Benedict Arnold. But he also sent the captured papers to General George Washington.

General Washington, with Lafayette and his staff, was approaching West Point. He had sent Colonel Alexander Hamilton on ahead to tell Arnold they were arriving early. General Washington told Hamilton, "I know you won't mind this task. You young men are all devoted to Mrs. Arnold."

After Hamilton delivered his message he sat down to breakfast with General and Mrs. Arnold.

While they were eating, a messenger came in and handed General Arnold the letter telling of André's capture.

When he read the news, Benedict Arnold's face did not change. He said, "I'll have to ask you to excuse me for a short time. A small emergency has come up. I will return shortly to welcome the Commander-in-Chief."

Then Arnold said to his wife, "I want to speak to you upstairs."

When they were alone he told her of André's capture. Arnold said he would have to flee for his life and that they might never meet again.

Peggy Arnold fainted.

Benedict Arnold kissed his sleeping baby boy, leaped on a horse, and rode down to the river. He grabbed a small boat and fled to the *Vulture*, which had come back up the Hudson in search of André.

An hour later George Washington arrived at Arnold's house. Almost immediately the messenger appeared with the papers that had been found on André. Mrs. Arnold's hysterical condition confirmed the messenger's terrible story.

Washington was stunned.

Turning to Lafayette, he exclaimed, "Whom can we trust now?"

George Washington was already in trouble. His men were being defeated and were deserting at every turn. Now, to top it all, one of his best generals, commanding a most important post, had gone over to the enemy. No one knew how deep the conspiracy went. No one knew who was friend or foe at West Point. But everyone now knew a British attack could be expected at any moment.

In this crisis at West Point, Washington showed the kind of leader he was. He brought in reinforcements, transferred men to break up any possible traitorous groups, and prepared to fight to the last gasp.

The attack never came. The reason was simple. Washington himself had the captured papers outlining the plans for the British assault. But Washington, of course, had no way of knowing that his was the only copy.

General Washington did not wish to punish André alone. Arnold was the man he wanted. Young Alexander Hamilton even wrote the British and tried to exchange Major André for General Arnold, but the attempt failed.

André was tried as a spy. There was no defense. The evidence was crystal clear. The laws of war have but one penalty for the captured spy.

Major André wrote Washington a letter asking to be shot like a soldier, not hanged like a criminal. He received no reply.

On October 2, 1780, nine days after his capture, twenty-nine-year-old Major John André dressed himself in his full British uniform (which his servant had been allowed to bring him) and walked up the steps to the scaffold. With great calm, he adjusted his own handkerchief over his eyes and the rope around his neck. He died with perfect courage.

André's fate aroused universal sympathy. The whole British army went into mourning for him. A tablet to his memory was placed in Westminster Abbey, London, the shrine of British heroes.

The three patriots who had captured André received gold medals from their government inscribed, "The love of country conquers."

Benedict Arnold was received into the British

Army as a brigadier general. He wrote General Washington an incredible letter saying that he felt he had always acted in the best interest of his country. He asked Washington to send him his things and to make sure that no harm came to Mrs. Arnold. Then he signed the letter: "Your obedient servant, B. Arnold."!

General Arnold fought against his fellow Americans and tried to get other Americans to follow his example and desert. After the war he and his wife and children lived in England. Much to his surprise, Benedict Arnold was shunned by the British because he was a traitor. He died at the age of sixty, a sad and lonely figure.

The man who betrayed West Point also betrayed himself.

Washington Monument at West Point

A ROCKY START

President George Washington selected West Point as the best site for a military academy. He urged Congress to build a school there for the training of future officers.

The last official letter ever written by Washington was to Alexander Hamilton about the importance of a military academy to our country. Two days later Washington died. It would have made him happy to know that on March 16, 1802, Thomas Jefferson signed a bill founding the United States Military Academy at Washington's favorite post, West Point.

The new academy got off to a rocky start with only ten "gentleman cadets."

There were no textbooks, no regular courses, no discipline. Cadets lived in a Revolutionary War barracks and had their meals in nearby houses, attended classes when they pleased and took long vacations whenever they wished.

The first Superintendent, Colonel Jonathan Williams, was discouraged. He called the Military Academy "a foundling barely existing among the mountains."

Colonel Williams and the next Superintendent, Colonel Joseph Swift (who had also been the first cadet to graduate), were made responsible for the fortification of New York City. As a result, they were away from West Point a large part of the time. So they had to entrust the management of the Academy to Captain Alden Partridge.

Partridge was a rugged man with a face that looked as though it were carved out of the granite from his native Vermont. A stiff officer, he was never seen out of uniform and never left the post. The cadets called him "Old Pewter," perhaps because of his fondness for the gray uniforms which he introduced at the Military Academy.

Captain Partridge was an able professor, a hard worker and a good drillmaster. He established regulations for parades and drills and had a military band ordered to the post. He started the cadet mess and some of the customs that are still followed today, such as marching to meals. He was very fond of infantry field exercise and the smallest details of the manual of arms.

But although he had his virtues, Captain Partridge had his faults as well. He employed many of his relatives, which later brought on official criticism. Cadets were admitted at any age (one was thirty-two and married; another was eleven). No entrance examinations were held. And Partridge did not get along with the faculty.

"Old Pewt's" favorite cadets graduated whenever he felt like recommending them for commission. When the cadets wanted anything, they sent him round-robin letters—letters with the signatures in a circle so he could not know who signed first. What the cadets asked for, they frequently got.

The Academy was five years old when a twenty-one-year-old Dartmouth graduate named Sylvanus Thayer entered. Partridge did not know it, but the name Thayer would one day spell "trouble" for him.

Thayer was the opposite of "Old Pewt." He was a handsome lad with fair skin and reddish hair. He was a student of military history. His hero was that firebrand of the day, Napoleon Bonaparte.

Sylvanus Thayer found the cadets living in crude quarters. The textbooks were elementary. But he enjoyed meeting such leaders of the day as Chief Justice John Marshall, DeWitt Clinton, and Robert Fulton, who gathered at West Point to discuss scientific matters at the meetings of The Military Philosophical Society, which young Thayer was asked to join.

After one year's "study," Thayer graduated. The next year he returned to West Point to be an instructor but at the outbreak of the War of 1812 he left West Point to fight. Thayer witnessed many American defeats brought on by jealousy among the officers, poor scouting work, and ignorance of warfare, and he resolved to dedicate himself to the improvement of the American army.

Sixty-five West Pointers fought in the War of 1812 (which lasted not one year but three). Ten were killed in action.

During that war the Military Academy almost closed for good. When Cadet Charles Merchant reported, he found that he was the only student and Partridge the only instructor. The future of West Point appeared doubtful.

After the war General Swift tried to persuade Congress to vote money to improve the run-down conditions. But men in Congress were beginning to think the Military Academy was a mistake and they sent no money. So Swift borrowed $65,000 from a New York merchant and built some of the fine stone buildings that are still used today.

But Swift was unable to spend much time at West Point. Meanwhile Partridge's disputes with the faculty were multiplying. Finally the faculty wrote Secretary of War James Monroe and said something had to be done about Partridge.

Monroe made an inspection trip to West Point. After observing conditions there, he decided Partridge should leave. But General Swift pleaded for his friend and Partridge was allowed to stay.

As soon as James Monroe became President, he made another trip to West Point. This time he found the faculty in revolt. The Professor of Mathematics greeted the President with a sealed letter listing all the bad things he said Partridge had done. It was signed by the faculty.

President Monroe's anger blazed. He called a court of inquiry.

Then Monroe did a wise thing. He ordered Sylvanus Thayer to West Point to become the next Superintendent. By choosing Thayer, Monroe shaped the character of West Point for all time.

Captain Partridge was beside himself with rage at the faculty's charges.

As soon as the President left, Partridge placed every member of the faculty, except one, under arrest. The cadets, all but forgotten in the heat of the moment, did exactly as they pleased.

West Point was in chaos.

This was the situation that greeted young Major Thayer when he arrived to take command of the Military Academy.

Grant Hall, West Point, New York

MUTINY
ON THE PARADE GROUND

Major Thayer was horrified by the conditions he found at West Point.

He found cadets drinking and gambling and lounging about the post.

Many were heavily in debt.

Cadets who had displeased Partridge were being punished by "cannon riding"—that is, sitting

45

astride a gun—in front of his quarters. Others were being marched about the Plain with signs on their backs. Thayer even found a few cadets locked in the "Black Hole," an underground prison.

There were supposed to be 240 cadets at the Academy, but many of them had taken vacations and no one knew when they would return.

Most of the cadets were doing exactly what they wanted to do.

On his arrival, Major Thayer marched into Captain Partridge's office and handed him a letter. As Partridge read the letter, he became very angry. The letter said:

> "Captain Alden Partridge, West Point.
>   On receipt of this you will deliver to Major Sylvanus Thayer, U. S. Engineers, the command of the Post of West Point and the superintendence of the Military Academy.
>   J. G. SWIFT, BRIG. GEN."

Late that night Partridge left the Academy without saying a word to Thayer. The ousted officer did not consider himself beaten. He had every intention of returning.

Meanwhile, Sylvanus Thayer set to work with a

will. He had an advantage over Partridge in that he had seen a great military academy in action in France. Partridge had been doing his best but with no example to guide him.

Thayer's first move was to write the Secretary of War to find out if he had the authority to reorganize West Point.

The reply was absolutely clear: "As Superintendent you are subject only to the orders of the President."

This was what Thayer wanted. At once he released the faculty from arrest, canceled all leaves, and ordered the cadets back to the post.

There was much to be done, and much to be undone. Thayer was determined to put West Point on a par with the military colleges he had visited in Europe. But in the middle of his reorganization something happened that must have shocked the hard-working Major.

One day, sitting at his desk, he heard wild cheering. He did not have to be told what had happened. He knew. Alden Partridge had returned!

Partridge stalked into Thayer's office and demanded his house back. Thayer refused. Then Partridge had an order read out to the cadets at parade saying that Captain Alden Partridge was once more Superintendent of West Point.

Thayer's heart must have sunk when he heard the cadets yelling. They were delighted to have Partridge back. They longed for the "good old days" when studies were simple and leave was automatic.

Sylvanus Thayer did not know what to do. Should he try to force Partridge to leave? Should he try to out-stay Partridge? Or should he himself leave?

Grimly he sat down and wrote to the Secretary of War: "I have the honor to inform you that Captain Partridge of the Corps of Engineers has returned to this post and has, this day, forcibly assumed the command and the superintendence of the Academy. I shall therefore proceed to New York and wait your orders."

Thayer mailed the letter and left.

He had acted cautiously and wisely. If he had stayed and tried to expel Partridge the excited cadets might have risen to defend him. This would have been mass mutiny, instead of one-man mutiny. And a mutiny of the entire Corps, at this critical time when the young Military Academy was struggling to get started, probably would have wrecked the institution forever.

The Secretary of War acted swiftly. An officer was sent to West Point with a message for the mutinous Partridge: "You will deliver your sword to the bearer . . . and consider yourself under arrest."

Thayer returned to resume command of West Point. And Alden Partridge—just ten days after his "revolution"—departed by steamboat for New York. Partridge was escorted to the wharf by the band and many sympathetic cadets. They put on a wild demonstration. By so doing, the undisciplined cadets were only making a bad situation worse.

General Winfield Scott presided over the court that tried Alden Partridge. Partridge was court-martialed on charges of mutiny, misconduct, contempt toward his commanding officer, disobedience of orders, and neglect of duty.

He was found guilty of insubordination only and was sentenced to be dismissed from the service.

Later, the President gave him a chance to resign instead, which he did. Partridge immediately preferred charges against Thayer and Swift, but President Monroe refused to consider them.

Alden Partridge spent the rest of his life writing attacks on his beloved West Point and the Regular Army. One pamphlet he wrote was called *The Military Academy at West Point Unmasked; or Corruption and Military Despotism Exposed.* It helped start a move in Congress to abolish West Point.

After the court-martial, Sylvanus Thayer wrote General Swift that things were straightened out and he expected no more difficulties.

True, Superintendent Thayer had successfully overcome mutiny. But little did he guess what other troubles lay ahead for him and the young Military Academy.

Exterior of Thayer Hall, West Point, New York

COLONEL THAYER, FATHER
OF THE MILITARY ACADEMY

Thayer's life, during his sixteen years as Superintendent at West Point, was filled with a series of crises, any one of which would have discouraged a less stout-hearted man and wrecked the young Academy. He rode out each storm with courage.

When Colonel Thayer took over West Point it was little more than a secondary school. By today's standards the entrance requirements were pitifully low. A candidate had to know only the three R's ("readin', writin', and 'rithmetic") to get in. And that was about all the average boy in this country learned in 1820.

Cadets were graduated at irregular intervals, as West Point had not yet adopted its four-year course. The cadets were, in a sense, "on tap." That is, when the army needed lieutenants, cadets were graduated to fill the need.

Sylvanus Thayer took a careful look at the situation, then set to work.

He discharged some ignorant cadets who had become known as "Uncle Sam's bad bargains." He established a rule that no boy could enter West Point unless he had finished high school.

In those days a high school education was expensive. So people began to call West Point "a retreat for pampered sons of the rich."

Some Congressmen wanted to do away with the Academy. Luckily, President Monroe stood firmly in favor of West Point and nothing came of the Congressmen's demands. Later President Andrew

Jackson declared: "It was for the descendants of those Revolutionary parents who died poor that the Military Academy was established."

Andrew Jackson and Sylvanus Thayer clashed over this idea—and many others.

Thayer was dedicated to the three D's of the fighting man:

> DISCIPLINE
> DECISION
> DEVOTION TO DUTY

These three D's came naturally to him. He had a methodical New England mind. He was austere and precise and always courteous. He moved quickly to get things done. (The cadets said, "Colonel Thayer waits for no man.")

One of Thayer's cadets, Francis H. Smith—the famous first Superintendent of Virginia Military Institute—wrote: "No cadet ever saw Colonel Thayer smile."

Thayer had a fabulous memory and cadets who appeared before him were surprised to find that the Superintendent knew their lives intimately. In the basement of the present Superintendent's quarters he administered the smallest details of cadet life, keeping all the records in his desk.

Francis Smith recorded this picture of Thayer: "One of my classmates presents his pass book for an order for 4 shirts. Colonel Thayer glances at the treasurer's balance sheet, always on the table, closes the pass book and hands it back to the cadet. The poor fellow was in great need . . . 'Colonel, I am much in need of shirts.'

" 'I take it for granted you are, or you would not present this order; but you are in *debt*.'

" 'But Colonel, I am almost destitute; I have only one shirt to my back and that is a fatigue jacket.'

" '*Well, Mister Dewey, I would advise you to wear that fatigue jacket until you are out of debt*.' "

Thayer was more concerned with making good officers than with making himself popular. He said, "All training for the military profession is useless without character building." He instituted many restrictions. Cadets were forbidden to marry. No cadet could possess a book of fiction. Newspapers were not allowed, except by special permission. No unnecessary conversation was permitted at mess. Cadets received $16 per month and an allowance of two rations per day.

Many ideas Thayer established are still in effect at West Point. Two of the most important are: "There will be no more than 15 men in a class" and "Every man will recite every day in every subject." Thayer founded the present grading system and laid the stones of the Honor System. The Honor System, which is administered by the cadets themselves, holds that no cadet will lie, steal or cheat—and any cadet who does so will be dismissed.

Thayer also created the Department of Tactics, headed by the Commandant, to run a fair— although Spartan—military program. But in the choice of his first Commandant, Sylvanus made one of his few mistakes. He chose Captain John Bliss.

Thayer wrote Secretary of War Calhoun that Bliss was "peculiarly well qualified to fill that im-

Statue of Colonel Thayer, "Father of the Military Academy." In the background is Washington Hall, the cadet dining hall.

portant station." But it turned out that Captain Bliss had a fault that made it hard for him to lead young men. He had a fiery temper.

One Sunday at parade, Captain Bliss's temper exploded. Cadet Edward Nicholson was misbehaving in ranks. Bliss seized him by the collar and jerked him out of the formation. Some said Bliss struck the cadet. All agreed he publicly cursed Nicholson. The cadets were furious.

Five cadets went to Colonel Thayer. They said, "We have been selected by the Corps to present to you this petition against Captain Bliss. We demand his removal." They tried to hand the Superintendent a petition signed by 179 cadets.

Thayer refused to accept the petition. He would not even look at it. He wanted no part of "Old Pewt's" rule by round-robin letter.

"Any cadet who feels himself aggrieved," said Thayer, "shall have a hearing. What you propose, however, is something else. It is unmilitary. You have my permission to go, gentlemen."

The next day, to Thayer's surprise, the committee returned. They tried once more to present the petition, plus a list of charges against Captain Bliss.

He was accused of hurling stones at cadets, throwing one cadet off the railing of South Barracks and another out of his room.

Thayer was furious. He ordered the five cadets to leave the post and he published an order to the Corps denouncing the petition procedure as "a crime of the first order."

This affair caused much excitement throughout the country. A court-martial was called by President Monroe, but no action was taken, on the grounds that cadets were not under military law. The five cadets appealed to Congress and to President Monroe, but got no satisfaction.

Captain Bliss was relieved by Secretary of War John C. Calhoun for not having "sufficient command of his temper." All five cadets were censured but allowed to resign. When it was all over, Colonel Thayer received a letter from the Secretary of War backing him for the stand he had taken. But one of the ringleaders, Cadet Andrew Jackson Donelson, developed a great hatred for Sylvanus Thayer which was later to result in trouble for the Superintendent.

This upheaval had far-reaching results. The

Corps of Cadets was officially made a part of the armed forces of the United States, subject to the Articles of War and to trial by courtmartial.

Colonel Thayer found a fine officer to replace Bliss as Commandant. He was Major William J. Worth. Worth was a fighting man. He fought the Chippewas and the British and he was later to write history with his sword during the Mexican War. He was a perfect soldier—tall, alert, and self-controlled. When he cantered his long-tailed horse across the parade ground he looked the dashing officer he was, and the cadets were proud to have him as their leader.

The Corps called Worth "Haughty Bill" but they liked him. He was strict yet impartial. They responded to his program for putting snap into the cadet drills and parades. It was Worth who developed the erect bearing that marks the men of West Point. Major William Worth left his stamp on the Tactical Department just as Thayer left his on the academic system.

The Long Gray Line was beginning to fall into step.

Exciting events crowded in on Thayer. Lafayette visited West Point and was royally entertained by the Superintendent. Although Sylvanus was a bachelor, he was known as a gracious host, thanks in part to his famous Irish cook, Molly.

Cadets came to West Point, studied under Thayer, and graduated to carve their names on the pages of history. Among them were George Washington Whistler, the famous railroad engineer chosen by the Czar to build the railroad from Moscow to St. Petersburg; Major David Moniac, a full-blooded Creek Indian, who was killed leading the attack at the Battle of Wahoo Swamp; Dennis Hart Mahan, the famous West Point educator who "never saw a battle and never went for a walk without an umbrella," yet was one of the best military minds this country ever produced; and Henry DuPont, founder of the DuPont empire. West Point was coming up in the world.

Many of Thayer's cadets later became famous Civil War leaders—men like Jefferson Davis, Robert E. Lee, Albert Sidney Johnson, Leonidas Polk, Joseph E. Johnston, and Philip St. George Cooke.

When Andrew Jackson became President, storm clouds gathered over West Point. Jackson disliked

Thayer intensely. There were several reasons for this. For one thing, Thayer was a fellow townsman of John Quincy Adams, whom Jackson hated. For another, Thayer had been sponsored by John C. Calhoun, whom Jackson also hated. Moreover, Thayer was a close friend of Jackson's enemy, General Winfield Scott. Added to all this was the fact that the President's private secretary was Andrew Jackson Donelson, who, because of his part in the Bliss affair, still hated Thayer.

The dislike between Thayer and the President soon came to a climax. Several cadets who had been dismissed from the Academy were sent back to West Point "by order of President Jackson." Colonel Thayer was indignant.

Then there was the episode concerning Cadet Alexander Wolcott of Connecticut. Wolcott, who had set fire to the icehouse, was tried and found guilty of arson and desertion—but his prison sentence was mysteriously changed to plain dismissal.

It was still another episode that brought matters to a head. Thayer felt that Cadet H. Ariel Norris was insubordinate, for during Andrew Jackson's campaign for reelection, Norris stole out after taps and planted a hickory pole in the center of the parade ground as a salute to "Old Hickory." Cadet Norris was taken to task by Colonel Thayer.

When Jackson heard of this he thundered, "Sylvanus Thayer is a tyrant."

Thayer received a reprimand from the President.

Soon Cadet Norris let it be known that he could act as he pleased at West Point. And one day, stimulated by presidential support, he loaded a metal candlestick, rammed in some full-dress bell buttons, and fired on a tactical officer passing beneath his window. This time Andrew Jackson did not come to the aid of Cadet Norris, who was tried and dismissed.

Thayer was beside himself over Jackson's constant undermining of his authority. He sent Ethan Allen Hitchcock—who had replaced Worth as Commandant—to tell the President that the rules must either be changed or enforced.

Thayer himself wrote the Secretary of War saying it was impossible to run West Point when "a dismissed cadet can get reinstated, whether by influence of powerful friends or by direct personal application to the President."

Then Sylvanus Thayer took a drastic step. He sent his resignation to the President. And Andrew Jackson accepted it.

West Point rocked with consternation. The Commandant handed in his resignation as a protest.

The men of the Corps were shocked and many came to call on Thayer to tell him good-by. A meeting of the faculty was held and it was decided that a portrait of Sylvanus should be painted, to be presented to him by the staff. When Thayer heard of this, for once he lost his calm poise.

"Gentlemen," he said, his eyes filling with tears, "I cannot permit such action. Under the circumstances it could be considered only as a reflection on President Jackson."

Colonel Thayer wanted to be certain his departure would be dignified, and not a rowdy exhibition like that which took place when "Old Pewt" left. Accordingly, Thayer would not tell anyone when he was going to leave. And to further his plans, each evening he would walk down the big hill to the Hudson River and watch the passing boats.

One night at dusk he was talking to several offi-

cers on the dock when the river boat's whistle
blew. Sylvanus held out his hand.

"Good-by, gentlemen," he said calmly. He
shook hands with each officer and then stepped
quickly aboard, leaving a surprised little group to
watch the paddle wheels of the steamer churn out
of sight.

Thus it was that Sylvanus Thayer, the father of
the Military Academy, left West Point forever.
But his spirit still guides the cadets.

The gymnasium at West Point

DANGEROUS JOURNEYS

One of Colonel Thayer's cadets was a tall boy from Massachusetts named Randolph Marcy. Marcy became one of the really great frontiersmen of the early West.

This cadet, like many boys today, read everything he could about the West and dreamed of the day when he would be a lieutenant on the frontier.

After his graduation, Marcy received the assignment he had hoped for, and what he saw out West amazed him.

He saw green travelers heading for wild country with little idea of the perils ahead. He saw wagons breaking down because they were overloaded, or because they were the wrong type for a rough overland journey. He saw families parched for lack of water in the waste-lands. He saw pioneers crossing Indian country in wagon trains, with no idea how to protect themselves from the savages.

Marcy found the trail westward littered with heavy furniture, pianos, and valuable household goods. He met emigrants traveling singly and in pairs, not organized to meet danger. Few knew how to take care of their animals. Few knew how to lay out an outpost at night or what to do in case of trouble.

The veterans on the plains were laughing at these poor people. Marcy wondered why the old-timers didn't share their knowledge with the new-comers. This gave him an idea: Why not get the experienced frontiersmen to write a book warning travelers of the dangers and giving them helpful advice? But most of the veterans did not know how to write.

"I just ain't educated," said Joe Snakerunner. "I know what to say but I don't fancy writin'."

Marcy decided that here was a chance to use all he had learned in four years under Thayer. He tightened his pistol belt.

"I'll write the book myself," he announced, "and you're going to help me, Joe Snakerunner."

Marcy called his book *The Prairie Traveller*. It told people crossing the plains how to organize into companies, what they should take and what they should leave behind, what to do when the Indians attacked, how to scout the enemy, how to prepare camping sites, and what kind of animals could best stand the trip.

"Take oxen, don't take horses," Marcy wrote.

Then he outlined the best routes westward.

Later, as a captain, Marcy traveled through the West exploring for the best routes for building roads. Marcy's West Point engineering helped him when he led his party through deep snows of the high Rockies. His work in blazing the trails and surveying routes aided thousands of people who trekked West in the Gold Rush days of 1849.

Colonel Thayer was proud of Cadet Marcy, one of the first of his boys to help our Country.

Another of Thayer's cadets was also an extraordinary writer. He has been called America's first real genius. His name was Edgar Allan Poe.

Poe came to West Point for one reason: to get a free education. He was not fitted for military life. He was a poet and the creator of the detective story. His vivid imagination began to show when he wrote his foster-father that he was the grandson of General Benedict Arnold!

Poe's life at West Point was the most baffling detective story of all. Six months after entering he wrote that he was doing well in his studies and was delighted with Colonel Thayer.

Less than three months later, this same cadet was being tried for "absences from parade and roll calls" (he pleaded not guilty) and "disobedience of orders" (he pleaded *guilty*). The mystery of this sudden change in conduct has never been solved.

The moody Cadet Poe drank a great deal. He

spent much of his time tippling at Benny Havens's Tavern in nearby Buttermilk Falls. This was a favorite after taps spot of the cadets and was, of course, off limits. Poe called Benny Havens "the only congenial soul in this God-forsaken place." It was a relief to both West Point and Edgar Allan Poe when Poe was dismissed.

Although West Point officers frowned on Benny Havens's Tavern, they allowed cadets to drink on special occasions like the Fourth of July and Washington's birthday.

Later liquor was outlawed forever at the Military Academy, but natural high spirits have always been part of cadet life.

Probably the most elaborate joke ever performed by cadets took place in the 1800s. It was too bad Poe was not present to throw in the fancy touches.

A group of second classmen purchased a billiard table in New York City. It was shipped to Garrison, across the river from West Point. This posed a problem. How were they to get it across the Hudson?

The cadets' solution was daring. One midnight

they loaded the billiard table on an ox-cart and pulled it across the rough river ice. A sound-proof home had already been prepared for the table in a coal room in the 6th Division of barracks.

The cadets went to work and equipped their billiard room with furniture, pictures, a barrel of cider, a barrel of crackers, and cheese. The owners of the table charged other cadets ten dollars a year to enjoy the privileges of the room.

Ladies of the post heard about the billiard hideaway and teased the officers of the Tactical Department because they could not find it. After the table had been in operation for almost a year, two officers saw some cadets disappear through the coal room door. The officers decided to postpone their raid to the next night in order to let other Tacs in on it.

But the cadets got wind of the officers' discovery. And when the Tacs made their raid, they did not find a single cadet. Instead, they found the room in spotless order. Lamps had been cleaned and shined, a good fire was burning in the fireplace, and cheese and crackers had been set out for the raiders. There was a note as well:

Honored Sirs:

Thank you for delaying your discovery. Please make yourselves at home and accept this billiard table as a token of our esteem.

Your obedient servants,

THE CLUB

Lieut. George W. Crook, Cadet Phil Sheridan, and Lieut. John Nugen. Sheridan became a great cavalry leader and Crook a famous Indian fighter.

TRIAL BY FIRE

During the thirty years of peace after the War of 1812, people began to argue that the United States did not need a military academy. They said, "We hate wars, so we are against West Point."

Army men thought this was like saying, "We hate fires, so we are against the fire department."

Men in the Ohio legislature cried, "Let's abolish

West Point!" Tennessee passed a resolution saying the Military Academy was a place where a few sons of wealthy families were educated at public expense.

The Superintendent, white-bearded Captain Henry Brewerton, met criticism at every turn. People complained because West Point officers resigned to take better paying jobs. (There was great demand for the engineers, architects and surveyors which the United States Military Academy had trained.) So Congress passed a law saying that a cadet had to stay in the army four years after graduating.

Then people complained because appointments to West Point were not given out fairly, and Congress passed a law allotting one cadetship to each Congressional District in the United States.

The feeling against West Point continued to rise —until the Mexican War.

This war was fought over Texas. The Mexicans said it belonged to them. When President James Polk signed a bill making Texas a state, the fighting began.

West Point men went swiftly into action. Here

was their first real chance to prove what West Point training could do. Even the men who had resigned returned to fight.

The top leaders were not West Pointers. Neither General Winfield ("Old Fuss and Feathers") Scott, General Zachary ("Old Rough and Ready") Taylor, nor Colonel William ("Haughty Bill") Worth had studied there. But they found that Military Academy graduates were invaluable because of their technical skills.

On the long and bloody road to Mexico City there were many deeds of bravery and military skill by West Pointers. Some of the young heroes later became the great leaders of the Civil War.

A dashing cavalryman who graduated from West Point just as the Mexican War started was Lieutenant Thomas Jonathan Jackson. He told his men, "Always mystify, mislead, and surprise the enemy" —and he did just that. He became the very spirit of lightning warfare. His motto was: *You can be whatever you want to be.* And later, when he fought for the South in the Civil War, his nickname told how hard it was to overrun his troops.

Both sides called him "Stonewall."

The West Pointers who made their mark in Mexico included some whose names are famous in American history. Among them were William Tecumseh Sherman, with the look of a wild eagle in his eyes; Jefferson Davis, the fighting Scots-Irishman; George McClellan, brilliant and over-cautious; Jubal Early, gimlet-eyed and shrewd; and Joseph Totten, an old-timer from the class of 1805, brought to the front from his job as Chief of Engineers.

At the Battle of Buena Vista two former cadets, William McKee and Henry Clay (the latter a son of the famous statesman) were lanced to death leading charges against the Mexican horsemen. "Old Rough and Ready" Taylor yelled, "Double-shot your guns and give it to 'em!" And the guns of Braxton Bragg and Jefferson Davis saved the two-day fight.

The Mexican Army, under General Santa Anna, retreated with little to show for their losses except two captured 6-pounder guns.

Back at West Point the cadets thrilled with pride

over the news of the Academy graduates. They fired a 30-gun salute to honor the victory at Buena Vista, a victory which left the Americans in control of the northern part of Mexico.

After almost a year and a half of fighting, the Americans swept into Mexico City. They had won thirty battles and lost none. They had captured 40,000 prisoners and 1,000 cannon.

When Captain Simon Drum smashed into Mexico City he found two more cannon: the two brass 6-pounders General Santa Anna had captured. Today these field pieces stand guard at West Point, inscribed: "Lost without dishonor, recovered with glory."

The Americans held a victory dinner in Mexico City. General Winfield Scott rose and proposed a toast to the Military Academy. "Without the science of West Point," he said, "this army multiplied by four could not have entered the capital of Mexico."

Another victory celebration was held at West Point. Cadet Phil Sheridan, later to become a daring cavalryman in the Union Army, wrote his sister:

WEST POINT,
February 17, 1849.

Dear Sister,

We became cadets today and took the oath of allegiance . . . It was as all military proceedings are, very pompous. The officers of the Post with the Academic Staff, assembled in the library building. In the center of the room was placed a table, around which all the officers were each arranged . . . in full uniform, wearing swords also; it looked just like they were going to cut some body to pieces. Each cadet advanced up to the table, laying his hand upon the Bible, swore to *deffend his Country, his liberties* his *honor* and obey the *commands* of all *superior officers;* after which he kissed the bible and received his warrant as a Cadet . . .

I suppose you red in the papers . . . the reception of the 20 colors taken during the Mexican War, which happened 3 or 4 weeks ago. I carried a flag taken at Chaputopeck it was tattered by balls.

CADET PHIL. H. SHERIDAN

P.S. Excuse me for being pompous in signing my name.

Sheridan was a better fighter than speller! A hot-headed, magnetic Irishman, he was almost discharged from West Point for fighting an upperclassman. He was saved by his excellent cadet record.

Of the 523 United States Military Academy graduates who served in the Mexican War, 452 received citations. The Military Academy became the pet and idol of the nation. No longer would anyone dare call West Point graduates "holiday soldiers from an aristocratic and useless institution."

Men differed about the war itself. Ulysses S. Grant wrote: "The Mexican War was one of the most unjust ever waged by a stronger nation against a weaker nation."

Everyone agreed, however, that at long last George Washington's wisdom had been proved. This country did need, as he foresaw, a military academy to train officers who would be able to organize citizen soldiers and lead them to victory in time of war.

Gen. Robert E. Lee when he was Super–
intendent at West Point

A CADET FROM VIRGINIA

The steamboat whistled as it rounded Gee's Point.
A bell clanged and the engines slowed to half-
speed; overhead, the funnel poured out a cloud of
black smoke. A deckhand pointed for the benefit
of a boy standing at the rail.

"That's Constitution Island," said the deckhand,
nodding his head. "And right in there is the Chain

Cove. That's where they had a battery guarding the Great Chain in the Revolutionary War."

The boy felt his pulse quicken. He had traveled two hundred miles for this moment.

Up the river, to the north, was a breathtaking view. Green-covered hills rose sharply from the water's edge, channeling the river.

"That's Storm King Mountain," continued the deckhand, "and Crow's Nest is on the tiptop."

The boy in the bow was almost six feet tall. He had a sturdy build, black curly hair, and a wide smile. He looked up at the forbidding cliffs. If he were successful in passing the entrance examinations, West Point would be his home for the next four years. He knew that if he once got to be a cadet nothing could stop him from graduating.

The boat pulled up to the small pier and the boy put his valise on the dock.

The tag hanging from the valise read: *Robert E. Lee.*

Young Lee, who was destined to become one of the greatest military leaders of all time, shouldered his bag and walked slowly up the hill.

Across the Plain stood two stone barracks, an academic building and officers' quarters. To the right, on a high mountain, was a rampart of old Fort Putnam, still standing guard over West Point. Lee trudged across the Plain.

"Hey! *You!* HALT!" shouted a cadet as Lee neared the barracks.

No member of the aristocratic Lee family had ever been addressed in such a manner, but the cadet was apparently addressing him, so Lee stopped.

"What's your name, Mister? Where you from?"

"Suh, my name is Robert Lee, from Virginia."

"Go register at headquarters, Mister Lee, then come back here and I'll teach you how to say *sir.*"

Lee began his cadet service like every boy of that time, by purchasing furniture for his room. All water was hand-carried from a nearby spring. A fireplace in each room supplied all the heat there was during the bitter winters.

Young Lee easily became accustomed to the strict routine of cadet life. His father, Major "Light-Horse" Harry Lee, a hard, devil-may-care cavalryman who fought under Washington in the Revolution, had trained his son to obey orders.

This training was invaluable to the young cadet.

The cadets called Robert the "Marble Model" because he was always so neat and never got into any trouble. During his four years at West Point, Lee made a record which has never been equaled: *he did not receive a single demerit.*

Lee thought Superintendent Thayer was a fine teacher. The classroom work was of a high order and the young Southerner excelled in his studies. He did so well in mathematics that Thayer took him out of class and made him an assistant professor of mathematics.

Cadet Lee found the food at West Point wholesome but not fancy, and with very little variety. The main dish was beef, which was served cold at breakfast. Lee, used to hot biscuits at every meal, got fresh bread only twice a week.

One winter night Second Classman Lee was studying in his room when he heard shouts. He ran to see what was the matter. The sky was red and the air was full of smoke. Someone shouted, "Fire! Everyone outside!" The Long Barracks were burning. These were the quarters of the artillery enlisted men, who were called The Bombardiers. (Their wooden barracks stood not far from where Battle Monument now stands.) Lee and the other cadets tried to help put out the fire but the two-story building burned to the ground.

During his last year at West Point, Lee was made cadet adjutant, a coveted honor.

A strict tactical officer nicknamed "Old Hant" —because of the way he haunted cadet barracks— caught almost every cadet in the Corps breaking the rules at one time or another. But he never could find any regulation which Robert E. Lee violated. Lee did not smoke, drink or play cards. He was extremely serious about his military education and everything else.

When graduation day arrived, Lee stood number two in his class. He was commissioned a second lieutenant of engineers and served on the Mississippi River.

The big river was causing trouble at St. Louis, where it was changing its course away from the city. The mathematics Lee had learned under Colonel Thayer helped him figure out how to build a dam that would send the river back to its original course.

During the Mexican War Captain Lee studied Winfield Scott's tactics. Lee served Scott as a daring scout and as a tireless planner. He saw how General Scott handled large numbers of men and how bold plans can win battles. Years later these lessons served Lee well.

After the Mexican War, Robert E. Lee was ordered back to West Point to become the Superintendent.

As Captain Lee came up the Hudson on the river boat, he thought back to the young boy who had climbed the hill twenty-seven years before. He was glad to be back at West Point.

The cadets knew of Lee's record in the Mexican War and they did not expect him to be a lenient Superintendent. Like Thayer, Lee was a Spartan in matters of discipline. Once, when it was hard to get enough money to buy the cadets saddles for their riding lessons, he said, "If necessary the cadets can ride without saddles."

But Lee understood the real needs of the cadets. He started the custom of giving them leave in the summer, a very popular idea.

One of Lee's cadets was James Whistler.

"Curly," as he was nicknamed, was the type of cadet who worried his Superintendent. Whistler received demerits at every turn. He was brilliant, but he studied only when the fancy struck him. Whistler failed in chemistry and Captain Lee had to dismiss him from the Academy. After Whistler became a famous artist, he laughed at his attempt to become a soldier and said, "If silicon had been a gas, I'd have passed my chemistry exam. Who knows? I might have been a general instead of an artist!"

When the Civil War broke out Lee's heart was heavy. General Scott offered him command of the Union Armies but he refused. Scott used every argument to keep Lee in the United States Army but Lee felt he owed his first duty to his home state, Virginia.

So, after thirty-two years of distinguished service to the United States, Robert E. Lee sadly resigned his Army commission. He could not fight against his relatives, his children and his home. He was tortured by the decision but there could be no compromise with duty as he saw it.

In the Civil War, the North had the advantage

in numbers of men and in war supplies, but the South had Lee. He quickly became the hero of the Confederacy.

People soon had reason to remember something Winfield Scott said when Lee was a young West Pointer fighting in the Mexican War: "Lee is the greatest military commander in America. In case of another war, his life should be insured for five million dollars."

The various uniforms worn by cadets at West Point

DRUMS IN THE DISTANCE

War drums were rumbling in the distance and their echoes were heard at West Point. Hotheads at Benny Havens's argued whether or not a state had the right to withdraw from the Union. The question of slavery was a burning one. As the 1860s drew near, everyone realized that ahead lay a time of great trial.

The small United States Army of 13,000 men

had its hands full carrying out the government's poorly planned policies with the Indians. Many former cadets had fallen by arrows shot from the bows of the Sioux, Apaches, Navahos and other fierce tribes. The government, appreciating the value of a well-trained officer, raised the pay of a cadet from $24 to $30 a month.

At the Academy, instruction in horsemanship was going full-blast. The cavalry instructors, realizing the importance of horsemanship in the threatening war, reported cadets for such things as "failing to keep horse in ranks," "not holding reins properly," "slouching in the saddle," and "spurring horse cruelly."

But although life in the Corps was as strict as it had been in Thayer's day, cadets were enjoying themselves.

When a plebe walked post at night in the old summer camp near Fort Clinton, upperclassmen would rush him, attempting to take away the sentinel's rifle, bayonet, and his clothing. Occasionally a sturdy plebe would put an upperclassman in the hospital with a butt-stroke of his rifle.

Traditionally, upperclassmen have never laid

their hands on plebes, except in disarming them while on sentry duty.

Even the upperclassmen on duty as officers or non-commissioned officers of the guard joined in the rush when the army officers were not around. Cadet officers answered the sentinel's challenge of "Halt! Who goes there?" with flip answers like, "The Queen of Sheba in a suit of armor," or "The devil's chariot drawn by four mud turtles." The idea was to confuse the plebe.

The Corps was doing its work and having its fun—as it always had—but the beat of the war drums was getting louder.

Then Congress passed a law known as The Missouri Compromise which settled the question of slavery for the time being. But when cadets decided to debate the question, "Has a state the right to void an Act of Congress?" the Superintendent thought they were going too far. He stepped in and stopped the debate before it started.

One morning a Southern cadet on duty as officer-of-the-guard ordered the fifes to stop playing "Yankee Doodle." Cadets from both the North and the South resented this. They hoped war between the two sections of our country could be averted.

When the telegraph wires flashed the news of John Brown's raid on the national arsenal at Harper's Ferry, West Point was electrified. The father of one of the cadets was a prisoner of the fanatical John Brown, who had mistakenly thought his surprise attack would touch off a general uprising of the slaves.

The excitement in the Corps was terrific.

Then over the wires flashed the word that Colonel Robert E. Lee, commanding United States Marines, was battling John Brown and his men. Many Southern cadets denounced the Northern cadets.

Cadet Gibbes of South Carolina and Cadet Emory Upton of New York became so excited that they fought each other. The fight took place before a group of cadets in the First Division of barracks. To many who saw it, the fight seemed to foretell the War Between the States. Cadets began to realize it would soon be friend against friend, classmate against classmate.

Orders came from Washington sending the

West Point horse-drawn battery away from the Academy for the inauguration of President Lincoln. The battery was a favorite of every cadet. At reveille on the day of departure, the cadets watched it prepare to leave. When the captain commanded, "Forward! Guide right!" the cadets gave a farewell cheer. They hated to see that battery go, for most of the horses at West Point went with it. And some of the Southern cadets realized they soon might have to brave those guns.

Many Southern cadets began to resign.

When a cadet left it was customary to allow him to call the battalion to attention in the mess hall. One popular Southerner, the First Sergeant of Company "A," stood at the doorway and shouted, "Battalion, Atten-*tion!* Good-by, boys! God bless you all!" His classmates rose and escorted him to the dock, carrying him on their shoulders.

In April of 1861, the Confederates sent cannon balls roaring across Charleston harbor at Fort Sumter. The cannon balls did more than smash into the fort: the sparks which sent them flying ignited the war.

The split between the Northern and Southern

cadets was now wide open. When they heard about the attack on Fort Sumter, the Northerners gathered in the room of Cadet Harris of New York and sang "The Star-Spangled Banner." Listeners said the singing could be heard across the Hudson River.

Sad farewells were said. Lieutenant Fitz Lee of Virginia, one of the most popular men ever at West Point, went to each cadet and shook hands and said good-by before he left for the South.

As staunch as we are for the Union today, one must admit it took moral courage for the Southern cadets to resign and go home. It meant leaving friends and the career of which they had dreamed and for which they had studied so hard.

At that time there were 86 cadets from the Southern States. Of these 65 resigned, leaving 21 Southerners at West Point in the service of the United States. These Southern boys struggled with themselves, trying to decide whether to stay at West Point or go home to fight for the South. More than three-fourths of the graduates remained loyal to the United States, including 50% of those of Southern birth.

Battle Monument, a memorial to members of the Regular Army
killed in the Civil War.

The Class of 1861 received commissions as lieutenants two months early.

The new first class signed a request also asking permission to graduate early. They wanted to fight. The War Department approved, and graduated this class a month after the previous one. When they had received their diplomas, the new lieutenants traveled to Washington and reported in a group to aging General Scott, the Chief of Staff. They told the General that they were ready to serve, that they would not take the furlough they had earned.

President Lincoln came over from the White House and welcomed the class into the service. The President was glad to receive forty-five new lieutenants devoted to the Stars and Stripes.

Back at West Point instructors were being ordered away to join fighting commands. They were replaced by older men. Major Delafield, who had been a stern Superintendent sixteen years earlier, became Superintendent once more.

The drums were now crashing thunder-loud and the bugles were sounding the charge.

Soon the telegraph instruments clicked out the news of the Union defeat at the Battle of Bull

Run. There was great excitement in the Corps. Twenty-two new lieutenants who had just graduated from West Point were in that battle.

Many of the battle leaders on both sides in the Civil War had worn cadet gray. Now they were coming face-to-face as enemies in the fiercest struggle ever fought on this continent.

Old Cadet Chapel

THE MAN
THEY ALMOST FORGOT

Back of the battle lines, General Lee poked at the embers of a campfire. On the other side of the dying fire stood a man whose nose had the sharpness of an eagle's beak.

"That's all I know about the Yankee generals, sir," General Dick Ewell was saying. Ewell put on his black hat and fingered his whiskers. He added,

96

"There is one West Pointer, I think in Missouri, and I hope the Northerners won't find out about him. I mean Sam Grant. He was at West Point with me when I was a cadet. He's clear-headed, quick and daring."

The Confederate general was talking about a poor boy from Georgetown, Ohio, who came to West Point twenty-two years before the Civil War began. The name by which he is known is Ulysses S. Grant.

Much of the story of West Point is in the lives of its battle leaders. Grant became one of the greatest of these leaders, but he had a hard time getting there.

When a congressman appointed Sam Grant to West Point, people in his home town wondered why the congressman had not picked a more outstanding boy.

"I won't go," said young Grant when he heard of the appointment. But the sixteen-year-old lad changed his mind because he wanted to see Philadelphia and New York. On the way, at Harrisburg, he climbed aboard the first train he ever saw. It was such a thrill that he was glad he had decided to go to West Point. The train whizzed along at eighteen miles an hour. When Grant reached New York City, he took the steamboat up the Hudson River.

On reaching the post, Grant was lined up with other candidates in front of the treasurer's office. He was asked where his money was for the trip home.

By this time he liked the looks of West Point.

"I intend to pass the examinations," Mister Grant replied firmly. "I'll go home when I graduate."

The Superintendent at that time, Major Richard Delafield, was on the warpath in an effort to tighten discipline. Unlike Cadet Robert E. Lee, New Cadet Grant knew nothing about carrying out orders, so he received many demerits. And the strange military habit of *always* being on time troubled him. In addition to standing low in conduct, he did poorly in French, artillery, infantry and cavalry tactics.

But while Major Delafield was not popular with the cadets, he worked for one result that really appealed to Cadet Grant: he wanted each cadet to become an expert horseman.

The cadets went at cavalry and light artillery drill in earnest.

Cadet Grant quickly established himself as the best rider in the Corps. He worked out a powerful sorrel horse named York and they got better and better as a jumping team. One day the jump was put up higher than ever.

A cadet warned Grant.

"Better look out. That horse will kill you. That's a terrible jump."

"I can die but once," Sam replied.

Horse and rider dashed for the bar. Grant tightened the reins slightly, pressed with his legs, and the powerful York cleared the bar at five feet, six inches. Grant had set an Academy record.

On one occasion Cadet Grant barely escaped serious trouble. He and another cadet "borrowed" one of the Commandant's turkeys and were cooking it over the open fire which heated their room.

The Officer of the Night came in to inspect.

The two cadets sprang to attention in front of

the fireplace. The officer nodded and passed on. Later, Grant said, "I never knew whether that officer was kind-hearted or whether he had a cold and couldn't smell turkey!"

One of Grant's friends was "Old Pete" Longstreet, so called because he was one of the oldest men in the Corps. This handsome giant from Alabama became devoted to Grant. Another friend was Cadet Simon Buckner of Kentucky. Like many other cadets from the South, Buckner and Longstreet were shocked to discover that they had to black their own boots. There were no slaves to jump at a cadet's bidding. Later Buckner and Longstreet were pitted against Sam Grant in the War Between the States.

Before Grant graduated, "Old Fuss and Feathers" Scott inspected the cadets. Sam Grant, carrying a rifle, passed in review with the rest of the Corps. Years later Grant wrote, "As we marched past, I had a flash that some day I would stand in Scott's place."

In the Mexican War, the senior army officers got a glimpse of Grant's daring. At the Battle of Monterrey, when ammunition ran low, it was Captain Ulysses Grant who rose to the emergency. He jumped on his horse and, hanging low on the animal's neck, Indian fashion, galloped away at top speed. Bullets zipped about him, but Grant got through with the key message.

Eleven years of peacetime army life followed, then Grant became discouraged and resigned.

In 1861 when the Civil War broke out, Grant went from person to person trying to get a job in the army. He felt that he owed it to his country to fight.

But nobody remembered him.

Finally the Governor of Illinois was impressed because Grant just wanted a chance to fight. Others pestering the governor wanted a high command, but not Grant. This may have been the reason why the governor gave Grant more of a command than he had hoped for. He got a regiment!

Grant worked his men hard. He insisted that they carry out orders and be punctual. At the same time, he did everything he asked his men to do. Soldiers like that kind of leadership.

Ulysses S. Grant had the trait of applying himself to a problem until it was solved, and this dogged stick-to-it-iveness made him the greatest Union general.

He also was smart enough to learn by experience. In his first battle, at Belmont, Missouri, on the banks of the Mississippi, Grant made the mistake of ordering all his troops into the fighting at the start of the battle. He saw later that if he had had some fresh troops ready to attack at the crucial moment, he could have ruined the enemy. He always held out a reserve after that.

Ulysses S. Grant was very forceful and he let nothing stand in the way of victory. Once a Union general telegraphed him: "Do you realize that if I advance, my division will be wiped out?" Grant telegraphed back, "I am glad you understand your orders."

On the Tennessee River, near a log chapel called Shiloh, Grant's troops engaged in one of the hardest battles of the war. He lost ten thousand men in the battle, but his troops still believed in him.

President Lincoln, in his search for a general who could win, selected Grant and placed him at the head of the Union Armies. With Grant in command, the soldiers in blue fought harder than ever a.d attacked the Confederacy from several directior .

A year later the Southern armies were reeling, and finally General Lee sent a white linen dishcloth to General Grant as a sign of truce. It was the end of four years of fierce civil warfare—Americans against Americans.

The two great commanders met at a brick house at Appomattox. General Lee was dressed in his best gray uniform. General Grant apologized to Lee for his muddy boots and for his unkempt appearance. For a while the two generals sat alone—a former Superintendent of the Military Academy and a former cadet who had almost been forgotten.

Lee surrendered and expected the worst. But he was agreeably surprised. Grant's terms to Lee were the fair terms of a fair man. Grant allowed the Confederates to keep their horses for the spring plowing. Moreover, some of the Union soldiers had their rations reduced for a few days so that Lee's men might eat.

Lieutenant General Blackshear Bryan, Superintendent at the Military Academy, said almost a hundred years later, "There was a lot of West

Point at the conference table between Lee and Grant."

Indeed, not all friendships made at West Point were destroyed by the war. After it was over, Buckner, the Southerner of cadet days who fought for the Confederacy, and Grant, the Northern leader, went mountain climbing together in Mexico.

Four years after the surrender, Grant ran for President. Thousands of his men remembered his unselfish devotion to the Union. Their votes made the former cadet the leader of the nation.

President Grant liked to return to West Point and review the cadets. He did this often at graduation time.

He was the first West Pointer to become President of the United States, but not the last.

And when he died, his old friend from the South, General Buckner, was one of the pall-bearers at the funeral.

Third class cadets firing 105mm howitzers during their artillery training at Camp Buckner, West Point, New York.

BROTHER REJOINS BROTHER

Behind the Northern lines in the Civil War there had been occasional gatherings of former cadets to talk about days at the Academy. They reminisced and sang "Benny Havens," the song about the jolly tavern keeper who became a West Point legend.

But the best reunion West Point graduates ever

held was the one at the Academy soon after the end of the Civil War.

The return of the fighters for this reunion was a dramatic occasion. Southern officers made their first appearance at West Point since the outbreak of the war. The hard-fighting Colonel Ranald Mackenzie, whom General Phil Sheridan had called "one of my young tigers," led old graduates of both sides in a salute to the wounded.

It was an exciting time. Old friends exchanged war experiences. Classmates inquired for and received news about missing friends, some of whom would never return.

When the bugles blew to assemble the cadets for afternoon parade, Colonel Mackenzie formed the old "grads" behind the band and led the formation to the homes of the old professors. The fighters were cheered every step of the way. The column grew in length as professors and instructors joined in.

At the flagpole, former cadet John West, of Georgia, made a speech. West picked a topic both sides could properly appreciate: the treatment of prisoners. He asked that in future wars no prisoner should die or suffer for lack of food, clothing or medical attention. It seemed strange to some that a Georgian should talk of the horrors of a prison when one of the worst prison camps had been at Andersonville, Georgia.

But West was sincere. He had been shocked when Morris Schaff, of Ohio, answering his inquiry about a friend, Cadet Murray, said, "Our friend died hungry in a prison camp."

After West's speech Colonel Mackenzie took over again. "Fall in ranks!" he commanded. "Let's march to the chapel."

There the men who had charged against each other on the battlefield knelt and prayed together. Brother had rejoined brother in a true reunion. The band played the *Te Deum,* and the reunion broke up to the tune of *Auld Lang Syne.*

A new phase of West Point life had begun.

After the surrender at Appomattox, Congress passed a law making it possible for Union veterans to enter the Academy if they were still under twenty-five years of age. These newcomers amazed their fellow cadets. Many of the candidates wore beards, some had held ranks as high as captain, and some had received their cadetships for bravery in action.

For the cadets, the training was more stern than it had been before the war.

Cadet Hugh Scott, later to become Superintendent and Chief of Staff of the Army, wrote his mother: "I was reported for gazing about in ranks. I only turned my head once, but they gave me four hours with a gun and trimmings on the area. I think that is too much for such a small offense."

Officers reported cadets for such things as "unlawful distribution of apples in the area" and "unsoldierlike conduct—concealing himself in the fireplace so as to evade the officer of the day."

Cadets were not highly regarded. Cadet Scott wrote: "We received notice that seats would be given out in the following order at the concert:

1st	soldiers
2nd	servant girls
3rd	others
4th	cadets"

In those days some cadets were still sleeping on the floor, with one blanket over them and a comforter underneath. If it got very cold they could add the dirty laundry bag.

Soon after Alexander Graham Bell astounded the world with the invention of the telephone, some enterprising cadets rigged up a telephone line from the 1st Division of barracks to the 8th Division. But the young electrical wizards served punishment tours for their feat. Officers were not encouraging new methods of communication!

Sunday was not a free day. Inspections of rooms and equipment on Sunday was followed by parade. At these parades cadets passed in review twice, the second time at the double.

Punishments ranged from a few demerits to imprisonment in a light prison or, for more serious offenses, in a dark prison. Educators agreed that West Point was efficient, but they termed it the most severe course of its kind in the world.

Now West Point came under attack again. Newspapers and magazines wrote bitter criticisms of the resignations of the Southern cadets before the war.

The official answer of the Military Academy was that each graduate had made his choice in the honest belief that he was right and had fought for the belief. (The oath which a cadet took before the war emphasized the state from which he came but did not call for allegiance to the United States Government. A cadet promised to obey the orders of the officers over him, the rules of the United States Army, and the regulations of the Military Academy. Later that oath was enlarged to include allegiance to the Federal Government.)

The criticism eventually died down, and life at West Point went on. The Corps passed in review before many distinguished visitors, including President Grant. Mark Twain came and lectured on "English as She is Taught." The cadets laughed and yelled when the humorist, in his dry nasal tone, poked fun at the Chaplain, who was on the stage with him. The reason the cadets yelled and stamped their feet was because the Chaplain was also Professor of English!

When the Hudson was frozen, cadets were given

the privilege of skating up the river to Cold Spring and back.

Colonel Emory Upton presented to the cadet gymnasium five sets of boxing gloves, some Indian clubs and dumbbells.

In barracks, a serious form of hazing was going on. Plebes were made to render personal service to upperclassmen and to suffer other punishments, such as double-timing on the stairs, holding books or weapons out at arm's length until exhausted, and so on. The "Supe," at that time General Schofield, addressed the Corps on these violations of regulations, and his talk was so forceful that for a while hazing ceased.

But even though discipline was iron-hard, cadets still played pranks.

The 1880 style of saying "Happy New Year!" at West Point was to roll cannon balls down the iron steps in barracks. This made the tactical officers frantic.

One Tac ran up to the dependable cadet captain, George Goethals, who was later to become famous as the builder of the Panama Canal.

"Mister Goethals!" shouted the Tac. "Who is

that man up there rolling those cannon balls?"

"I don't know, sir," was the answer. "He's wearing a mask."

There were pillow fights in barracks after the bugle had sounded tattoo at bedtime. And in summer camp when lights were out, "ghosts" dressed in sheets appeared from all directions to frighten plebe sentinels. (One plebe who did not scare easily later became the leader of our armies in World War I. His name was John J. Pershing.)

The "Supe" found out about the "ghosts" and ordered the Tacs to see that strict discipline was maintained. As a result, the ghosts faded back into their tents.

Life for a new cadet in those days was rugged. Candidates arriving at West Point were made aware of this at once. They were greeted with this sign when they reported in:

```
TAKE OFF YOUR *HAT*
BUTTON YOUR COAT
SPEAK WHEN YOU ARE SPOKEN TO
KEEP YOUR MOUTH SHUT
KNOCK AND WAIT
STAY IN YOUR ROOM
THROW OUT YOUR CHESTS
SAY "SIR" TO SUPERIORS
```

George Armstrong Custer as a cadet

SABER VERSUS TOMAHAWK

Once when there was an Indian attack on the western frontier, General Winfield Scott said, "If this keeps up, I'm going to fight Indians and I'll take the first class of cadets along."

But the cadets did not get excited, for they knew that the old general was "just talking." The cadets realized it was their duty to stay where they were, to study and train to become officers.

During the War Between the States, word trickled back to West Point every now and then about Indian uprisings on the frontier.

The cadets had heard General Sherman say, "Young gentlemen, you think war is all glory and honor. It is not. War is hell."

But in spite of this famous warning, many cadets were eager for combat. They thought some West Pointers would probably have to fight the red men, and that is exactly what happened.

Back from the West came suggestions from officers who were meeting the Indians face-to-face:

"Have the cadets learn all about horses. Stress riding. Be sure they know how to break in a colt. Teach the pistol attack. Be sure they know how to charge with sabers. How to dismount quickly and fight on foot."

As a result, instruction in riding was increased and cadets galloped down dirt roads on both sides of the Hudson on cavalry maneuvers.

In the West the Indians were making a desperate stand to retain their territory. They saw their way of life vanishing. More and more white men were coming to mine the gold. Union Pacific workmen were laying steel tracks across the prairies for "the Iron Horse." And when men back in Pennsylvania found that buffalo hides could be made into excellent leather, thousands of white hunters went into Indian country to slaughter buffaloes.

The Indians tore down the "talking wires," as they called the telegraph. They waylaid the overland mail. Then they got bolder and attacked the soldiers who had been sent west to protect the white men.

An "Indian Fighting Army" was organized to deal with the situation. In this army, several former cadets stood out. Among them were George Crook, Ranald Mackenzie and George Armstrong Custer. All three had learned how to fight under General Phil Sheridan during the Civil War.

George Crook was a wise commander; one who saw the Indian's side of the problem. Whenever he could, he tried to settle arguments without bloodshed.

Ranald Mackenzie was a hard man to serve under because of the fierce punishments he dealt out. But once on the enemy's trail, he was a dynamic leader who did not know what it was to quit. He never lost a fight against the Indians.

George Armstrong Custer was a different kind of officer. He was promoted from captain to brigadier general in one jump, while his classmates were still captains.

Custer was a showman. He dressed in buckskin. He wore a broad black hat, a red bandanna handkerchief about his neck, and let his yellow hair hang down over the back of his collar. He wore red-topped boots, and white gauntlets covered his hands and wrists. Custer was vain, yet brave and daring. He was called "Glory Hunter" and the name fits him. Everybody in the country knew who Custer was.

That was one of his troubles.

Young General Custer took pains to see that his exploits and fights were written up in the papers.

When the Sioux, under their chiefs, Crazy Horse and Sitting Bull, gathered their forces for a showdown, Custer thought he saw a chance to add to his reputation.

His Seventh Cavalry Regiment was part of a larger force advancing into Sioux Territory. So anxious was Custer to find the enemy and close with them, that he split his regiment in three parts. This was dangerous. The separate columns might not be able to help each other. Now the enemy had a chance to defeat them one by one.

On the Little Big Horn River, Custer blundered into 2,500 Sioux Indians. Custer had only 265 soldiers.

In the battle all of the men under Custer's personal leadership were wiped out. The slaughter horrified the nation.

Custer's cadet friend, Tom Rosser of Texas, who had fought hard for the South in the Civil War, volunteered to go to the Little Big Horn to rescue Custer's body.

Longfellow, the poet, wrote that a Sioux chieftain, Rain-In-The-Face, had cut out Custer's heart. Then the story got around that the Indian had eaten it. But the truth is that Custer's body was not mutilated. When it was found, surrounded by his dead officers and men, observers noted that one bullet had pierced Custer's brain, another his body.

The government sent more troops into the field

and the "Indian Fighting Army" gradually wore down the savages.

Meanwhile, Custer's body was brought to West Point for burial. Two thousand people came down from Poughkeepsie for the funeral and boatloads came up from New York City. People were anxious to pay their respects to the "Last of the Cavaliers," as Custer was sometimes called.

At the funeral, one group of cadets formed as a battery of artillery. The rest marched as a battalion of infantry, carrying their arms reversed—muzzle down, trigger guard up—as a sign of mourning.

A detachment of cavalry led the funeral procession. Then came the cadet artillery battalion, followed by the United States colors and the colors of the Corps of Cadets, both draped in black. The band, with drums muffled, played the funeral march.

An artillery carriage, pulled by four black horses, bore Custer's coffin. Behind it came a trooper leading a horse with an empty saddle, a cavalryman's boots pointing backward in the stirrups. Among the pall-bearers was General Randolph Marcy, West Point's famous explorer.

The cadet riflemen fired three volleys over the grave to give General Custer his final salute. Then a bugler sounded taps.

The next day the cadets read these headlines in the *New York Herald:* "CHIEF JOSEPH, OF THE NEZ PERCÉS INDIANS, SURRENDERS."

Out on the plains the red men were beginning to realize the end was in sight—something they refused to do at the start of the clash between the saber and the tomahawk.

Michie Stadium at West Point

CADET MICHIE'S IDEA

There was little excitement at West Point in the 1880s. To one cadet, Dennis Michie, it seemed as if he had been born too late, for he had missed the stirring events of the Civil War and the breathtaking fights with the Indians.

While preparing for the Academy at Lawrenceville School, Denny had played football and liked it. He wanted to vary the cadet routine of study, drill, parade, and study. There were no athletics in those days except swimming instruction in the Hudson River and one hour a day of gymnastics.

Cadet Michie (pronounced *Mý-key*) decided to do something about the situation. He got the idea of having a cadet football team at West Point.

One reason athletics had been a long time coming to West Point was the difficulty of dress. For many years the principal uniform had been the bell-buttoned full-dress coat with its tight fitting collar. There was a more comfortable uniform for drill and for meals, but nothing suitable for sports.

One day Major Hamilton Hawkins, the Commandant of Cadets, saw some cadets playing ball in their full-dress coats.

"Are you young gentlemen wearing white shirts?" asked the Major.

"Yes, sir."

"Then," said the Commandant, "I authorize you to lay aside your jackets."

Eventually Michie's enthusiastic players bought their own uniforms and started playing the game in earnest.

The Navy had been playing football at Annapolis ten years before Michie entered West Point. The cadets were excited about Dennis Michie's idea because they hoped to compete against the midshipmen.

This small but dynamic cadet formed the first football team at the Academy, coached it, and played halfback. He was assisted by Leonard Prince, a boy from Illinois, who played right end.

Most of the college boys playing football then were giants—the style of play in Michie's day put a premium on big people—but that did not worry Denny. He weighed only 142 pounds but he liked the crash and excitement.

There was only one game the first season: *Navy*. One thousand people watched the game, which was played on the Plain at West Point. The heavier midshipmen ran their wedge plays with skill, and beat the cadets with a score of 24 to o.

Now the whole post became interested in football!

With six games scheduled for the next year, Denny and others felt they needed a more experienced coach. Doctor Harry Williams, who had been a famous player at Yale, said he would coach them for nothing, just to get a chance to beat the midshipmen. This was very agreeable to the cadets.

Denny and his teammates worked hard. The spirit at West Point backed the team and the midshipmen were beaten, 32 to 16. It was a sweet victory and it led to West Point's scheduling the best teams in the East. But the Navy game was still the most important one on the list.

For a mascot the midshipmen adopted a goat and later the cadets selected a mule. But the cadets did not know that often mules are afraid of goats. When the goat was introduced to the mule before the Navy game, the mule embarrassed the cadets by running away. Some said the smell of the goat bothered the mule.

Back at West Point the cadets secured a goat and put him in the same stall with the Army mascot. The two animals became friends. But in Philadelphia the next fall, when he met the Navy goat, the mule ran away again. He did not like the *new* goat! Finally the cadets got two mules that were not bothered by the smell of the goat, and the pre-game ceremonies became more pleasant for the cadets.

Twenty-three years after Dennis Michie graduated, a stocky, tow-headed Indiana Hoosier strutted into the area of barracks as a West Point candidate.

An upperclassman on the Beast Detail (upperclassmen charged with the training of new cadets) stopped him and asked what sports he played.

"Sir, I play football, baseball, basketball, boxing, track, swimming, handball and hockey."

"What's your name, Mister?"

"Elmer Oliphant, sir."

Elmer "Elephant," as he came to be called, not only played the sports he said he did, but he was a star. He became one of the greatest line-plunging halfbacks of all time.

Football was rougher in the early years of the sport. Under the rules, defensive linemen could hit their opponents with their open palms, and the West Point line coach, "Pot" Graves, believed in playing the rules to the hilt.

Graves had his linemen wrap their hands with black friction tape and bang the opposing players in the head. Every afternoon when the practice drill was under way, Graves would let out a yell.

"Blood! Blood! Blood! We've been practicing here for fifteen minutes now and I don't see any blood!"

This drill drew a crowd. Of course larger crowds came to see the games on the Plain. In 1920 there were so many people at the Army-Notre Dame game that some of the overloaded bleachers broke down. It was obvious to many officers on the post that West Point would have to build a permanent football stadium. A marshy meadow west of Lusk Reservoir was selected for the site and, after the field had been drained, construction started.

Not long after the stadium was completed, a husky red-headed cadet from Louisiana entered West Point. His name was Christian Cagle and the most descriptive word for his style of play is "spectacular."

"Red" Cagle, one of the fastest backs in the game, often reversed his field, running deep behind the line of scrimmage to scatter the opposing players. Then he would zigzag down the field or throw a forty-yard pass on the dead run. He made the spectators gasp.

Once when the West Point football team traveled by special train to Palo Alto, California, to play the Stanford "Indians," Biff Jones, the Army coach, stopped the train in the Arizona desert so the cadets could limber up.

A number of jack rabbits jumped out of the sage when the players got off the train, and the players chased them. No one knew exactly how fast Cagle could run, but that practice in the desert determined one thing: Cagle could *not* outrun a jack rabbit!

Cadet Cagle ran afoul of the rule that a cadet may have "no horse, no wife and no moustache." When it was discovered that Cagle had married, while on leave from the Academy, he had to resign.

West Point has had a long line of remarkable football players. Two of the greatest were "Doc" Blanchard, a six-foot, two-hundred-and-ten-pound cadet from South Carolina, and Glenn Davis, of California. Sportswriters called them "the touchdown twins." They played the game hard, the way Michie played.

Ever since Cadet Dennis Michie got his idea,

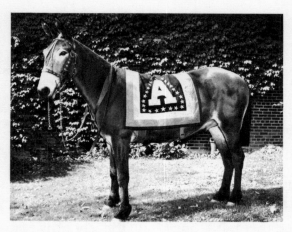

"Bud," the Army Mule. Each star on his blanket represents a victory over the Navy in football.

football has been the principal sport of the cadets at West Point.

The West Point stadium, tucked away in the hills below old Fort "Put," is well named. The plaque on the south tower reads:

MICHIE STADIUM
In Memory Of
DENNIS MAHAN MICHIE
U.S.M.A. 1892

Born at West Point, N. Y., April 10, 1870. Killed in action at San Juan, Cuba, July 1, 1898. In 1890 he organized and captained the first football team of The United States Military Academy.

Cadet John J. Pershing, Class of 1886

"X" MARKS THE SPOT

Charles Summerall, class of 1892, wrote:

"After we beat Navy in the second football game we got up class yells, and a marked change in discipline and in the relations between cadets and officers began to appear.

"Football teams from different colleges came to West Point and played our team. Their presence in the mess hall, their college yells at meals, and their non-military atmosphere were in strange contrast to the ancient customs of the Academy.

"When our team returned from beating the Navy, it was met at the train by the 250 men in the Corps and borne on their shoulders with such yells and pandemonium as the hills of the Hudson had never heard. We realized . . . that a new era had been ushered in."

When Charles Summerall was in the Corps, the regulations were unusually rigid. Cadets were not allowed to have money, to play cards or chess, to read novels, to play musical instruments, or even to smoke.

For excitement they used to enjoy something called the "Rush." Cadet Charles Rhodes described it this way: "Yesterday, the second class came back from furlough . . . The cadets formed in one long line on the Plain, and patiently waited for the steamer . . . Presently . . . a black mass appeared on the brow of the hill, hurrying forward toward camp. A signal was given and the two classes rushed at each other, fully an eighth of a mile apart, whooping, shouting and throwing up their caps. Every fellow seized and hugged some other fellow, and all were swallowed up in a dense mass of dust."

But the "Rushes" became so violent that the Superintendent announced that any cadet who took part in one would be dismissed.

At the turn of the century, West Point was like a rural village. Barns, chicken houses and gardens were everywhere. Most of the Academy buildings were old and inadequate. Cadet barracks were crowded and there were no comforts such as bathrooms or running water. The cadets had to use buckets to carry in all the water they needed.

Much of the social life at this time centered around the old West Point Hotel overlooking the Hudson River at Trophy Point. Many famous visitors stayed there. The place of General Scott as the fatherly "Old Army" advisor to the cadets had been taken by General William Tecumseh Sherman. The cadets liked to hear Sherman's humorous stories of his own cadet days and they were always impressed when he showed up at graduation exercises resplendent in his full-dress uniform.

When June, 1902, rolled around, the Military

Academy celebrated its hundredth anniversary with a three-day Centennial. Many toasts were drunk and the camp songs "Rally 'Round the Flag" and "Dixie" were sung to show that Civil War wounds were healing. There was a big Field Day and a baseball game with Yale. The celebration ended with a great banquet and fireworks.

President Theodore Roosevelt, who came to West Point for the Centennial, spoke about the place the Military Academy had made for itself in the first hundred years of its life. He said:

> "During that century no other educational institution in the land contributed so many names as West Point to the honor roll of the nation's greatest citizens."

As the new century began, American fighting men were grappling with the Chinese in the Boxer Rebellion. A Chinese secret society known as the Boxers swore to expel all "foreign devils" from China. They attacked the Christians and foreigners in Peking.

Many United States troops were shipped to China, as well as soldiers of other nations. Lieu-

tenant Charles Summerall went along as an artil-
leryman in the famous "Reilly's Battery."

The advance on the walled city of Peking was
under the worst possible conditions. The weather
was hot. There was a scarcity of good drinking
water. The Boxers had poisoned the wells, and
many dead bodies floated down the dirty stream
along which our troops advanced. The horses
were so thirsty they could hardly pull the guns.

During the attack, Summerall received an order from Captain Reilly to blow open the gates of
the wall so our troops could enter. Summerall's
artillery platoon wheeled into position fifteen feet
from one of the three gates. Our doughboys, on a
wall behind the battery, were firing over the
heads of the cannoneers at Chinese sharpshooters
who were on top of the wall ahead and in windows of the Forbidden City.

The platoon received rifle fire from the flank,
and men and horses went down. The noise was
terrific. The guns roared at the wall but the heavy
gates held.

Summerall's men and animals were in too dangerous a position to remain much longer.

Lieutenant Summerall ran forward and hurriedly scratched an "X" on the metal covering of the gate opposite the bars which reinforced it. Then he returned and ordered a gunner to fire at that spot.

Later Summerall wrote: "The gunner was Corporal Smith, from the mountains of Tennessee, and he had an accurate eye. The first high explosive shell cut its way through the gate and smashed part of a bar. I made two more scratches. . . . With two more shells the bar was cut and the gates swung open.

"Under the cover of my guns, the foot-soldiers of the 14th Infantry ran through the gates to the next wall. They placed some scaling ladders, which I had gotten from the Japanese, against the wall, and up they went into the city."

The Boxers were soon subdued.

There was a brief period of peace.

Then the First World War broke out, fifteen years after the Boxer trouble. The United States found itself opposing the troops of a greedy and ruthless German government.

We were poorly prepared. The demand for officers was great, but West Point was graduating fewer than two hundred men in each class.

Our Allies, who had been fighting the German armies for three years before we entered, had to hold the Germans for fifteen more months before we could place an army in France.

America was straining to get ready.

At West Point three classes were graduated early; the members of one class served only seventeen months as cadets. The "Supe" geared the training to a fast pace. This meant extra work and fewer privileges. The cadets did not mind the work because they knew serious dangers lay ahead, but they hated to have their summer leave cut to one month and their graduation leave reduced from three months to two weeks.

In France the situation was serious. The French nation was exhausted. Almost every day some Allied leader asked the senior American general, John J. Pershing, "When will the Americans be ready?"

General Pershing faced a great problem. He solved it by insisting that our troops *not* be fed into the British and French armies as replacements. He knew our men could fight better as a spirited unit under the leadership of their own officers. Finally the First Division entered the trenches on the Lorraine battlefront and showed the world how a well-trained American outfit could fight.

In the decisive battle of Soissons, Summerall, now a general, introduced a new tactic. Instead of spreading the guns out along the artillery line as was the custom, he massed many cannon behind two key infantry regiments. As a result, a rain of fire descended on the enemy trenches and our infantry was able to go forward and capture the German positions.

In showing how infantry and artillery can work as a team, Summerall made a valuable contribution to the American army.

When the fighters came home after the war, our nation honored General Pershing and his soldiers. The training Pershing had received as a cadet set the pattern in many a hard battle and he was quick to give much of the credit to the Academy. He wrote: *"The principles of warfare as I learned them at West Point remain unchanged."* He said

John J. Pershing, General of the Armies

he had applied these principles against the Indians in the West, the Spaniards in Cuba, and in World War I.

Because of his unusual leadership, Congress gave Pershing the title: "General of the Armies." No other American general has ever held this title.

After the close of the First World War, the great General came to West Point, and the Corps passed in review for him. Later, he shook hands with every cadet at a reception in the gymnasium. When one mother introduced her cadet son to him, Pershing spied a vacant buttonhole. The General's only greeting to the cadet was a tart: "Button up your full-dress coat!"

Then Marshal Foch came. The cadets were formed in a hollow square to hear the Supreme Commander of the Allied Forces. Foch, speaking only French, talked to the cadets through an interpreter. "I know your motto," he said. "Duty, Honor, Country. Your graduates lived up to this motto on the battlefields, and you will do the same."

Cadet Douglas MacArthur, Class of 1903

EVERY MAN AN ATHLETE

One January day in 1880 a sergeant entered the stables at Fort Little Rock, Arkansas, and addressed the men curry-combing the horses.

"Another Army Brat," he announced. "Captain and Mrs. Arthur MacArthur have a baby boy. Douglas is his name."

This Army Brat spent his boyhood with the soldiers of the Old Army—the "Indian Fighting

Army." On one occasion when the Indians attacked the fort, an arrow narrowly missed the four-year-old boy. Had that arrow found its target, our country would have been deprived of one of its greatest military leaders.

Douglas MacArthur accepted West Point life as if he had been trained for it. He was serious-minded about his duty, yet he had time for the activities of the Corps.

He enjoyed the physical training in the gym. He liked building pontoon bridges on the Hudson, under supervision of engineers. He excelled at the light artillery drill in which three-inch guns on wheels, drawn by horses, were whisked about the drill field at a gallop.

He enjoyed managing the football team and he scored a run in the first Army-Navy baseball game. He was a center fielder, fleet of foot, and he had a strong arm.

Cadet MacArthur, tall, slim and handsome, was a great favorite with the ladies. He was often seen strolling, with one girl or another, along Flirtation Walk. This is the romantic pathway that leads from Kosciusko's garden along the banks of the Hudson to the place where the Great Chain was anchored during the Revolution.

Flirtation Walk passes by the famous Kissing Rock. According to legend, the rock will fall if a cadet walks beneath it and does not kiss the girl with him. There is no record of Cadet Mac-Arthur's giving the rock the slightest tremble.

In MacArthur's last year at the Academy he was chosen to be First Captain. This was one of the few times in the Academy's history that the highest ranking cadet was also top man in his studies. Douglas MacArthur made an academic record that was unequaled for twenty-three years. (In 1926 Cadet William C. Baker, Jr., of Tennessee, beat it with the unbelievable scholastic average of 98.5%.)

Instead of concentrating on engineering after he graduated, as many brilliant scholars have done, MacArthur turned all his efforts toward being a soldier.

His first important chance came on the Mexican border. Pancho Villa, the Mexican bandit, had broken loose and our troops were patrolling the border. Young MacArthur dressed as a tramp and scouted behind the enemy lines. This was hazardous work; not every military leader would relish being alone in enemy country. But MacArthur came through it unscathed.

At the start of World War I, MacArthur's star began to rise spectacularly. He organized the famous Rainbow Division and led it against the Germans in France.

The long battle lines spread across south-western Europe. There were miles of trenches, and between the Allied and German Armies lay a strip known as No-Man's Land. Each army patrolled this territory at night to find out what the other side was going to do. The scouting was dangerous, but MacArthur was equal to it. For his work as a member of a patrol working in No-Man's Land, General Douglas MacArthur received his first Distinguished Service Cross.

After the war the Chief of Staff, General Peyton March, sent for MacArthur and ordered him to West Point as Superintendent.

March said, "West Point is forty years behind the times." He told MacArthur he was worried because the Military Academy had lost its spirit—

the spirit which had made its graduates great.

The fact was that World War I had disrupted life at West Point.

And once again some Congressmen tried to do away with the Academy. Certain graduates felt that it would never be the same. Both groups forgot to consider the adaptability of the cadets and the caliber of the new "Supe."

To reawaken the spirit at West Point, General MacArthur stressed athletics.

In France he had seen officers in poor physical condition who were unable to lead men properly. His aim was "Every Man an Athlete." He wanted to build bodies capable of withstanding the terrible strain of battle.

The General and Colonel Herman Koehler, Master of the Sword, organized the cadets who could not make the varsity teams into intramural, or company, teams. Later the idea spread to other colleges. MacArthur wanted to improve cadets physically and to develop athletes for the varsity.

As a result of his efforts, the Spirit of the Corps reasserted itself.

Later, the cadets referred to themselves and

their athletic squads as "The 1200 Mule Team."

MacArthur's interest in baseball and football was especially keen. He had Hans Lobert, the varsity baseball coach, report to him every Monday morning at nine o'clock to analyze the previous week's cadet games and to discuss the development of the players.

Almost every day the General was a spectator at football practice. When MacArthur, standing on the sidelines, told a player, "I want to see you make the tackle on this kickoff," that player felt as if he had wings on his feet.

One season, while practicing for the Navy game, the football coaches told the General they were handicapped by darkness. MacArthur ordered the soldiers of the Coast Artillery Detachment to install their huge searchlights on the ramparts of Fort Putnam, high on the hill above the Cadet Chapel. When the head coach wanted light, he spoke to the cadet manager, who fired a signal pistol into the air. The colored flare floated overhead and instantly the searchlights flooded the practice field with light.

Often in talking to his staff MacArthur called

attention to the West Point motto: DUTY, HONOR, COUNTRY. He said, "These are the words we must cling to in this changing world."

With all the responsibilities which came to him as a battle leader in World War II, Douglas MacArthur never lost his interest in Academy athletics. When MacArthur was Supreme Commander in Tokyo, Major Tom Mesereau, a recent graduate, reported to him.

"Why didn't Cadet Elmblad start the Navy football game?" asked the General.

The Major was startled. MacArthur, who had not seen an Army-Navy game in more than fourteen years, was well versed in the football situation!

In 1949, Cadet William Knapp, head cheerleader, wrote to the General, "I have been authorized by the Commandant to communicate with you regarding the Army-Navy rally this year . . . Will you send a message to the Corps?"

The General replied: "From the Far East I send you one single thought, one sole idea—written in red on every beachhead from Australia to Tokyo —*there is no substitute for victory!*"

General Douglas MacArthur signing the articles of surrender by the Japanese in World War II on the deck of the *U.S.S. Missouri*.

Because he has been a leader men would rally behind in times of peril, Douglas MacArthur has received nearly every decoration the free world has to offer. Yet he wrote from the Supreme Headquarters of the Allied Forces in Tokyo, on the occasion of West Point's 150th birthday:

> "Nearly 48 years have gone since I joined the long gray line. As an Army 'brat' it was the fulfillment of all my boyish dreams. The world has turned over many times since that day and the dreams have vanished through the passing years, but through the grim murk of it all, the pride and thrill of being a West Pointer has never dimmed. And as I near the end of the road what I felt when I was sworn in on The Plain so long ago I can still say— 'that is my greatest honor'."

Cadets leaving class at Thayer Hall

A CADET CALLED IKE

Dwight David Eisenhower was the third child in a family of seven boys. The Eisenhowers were very poor. Dwight's mother said, "Ike, if you want an education, go out and get one."

Ike tried to get into the Naval Academy when he was twenty years of age but found that he was too old. He took the competitive examinations for West Point, given by Senator Bristow of Kansas, and received the second highest marks. His army career might well have ended then—even before it began. As it happened, however, the man who came in first decided that he did not want the appointment. On such small decisions, history turns.

Ike's mother was a woman of strong character who reared all her boys to be fine men. She knew the value of a West Point education. When Ike said he wanted to go into the army, Mrs. Eisenhower agreed, but cautioned, "Never forget that they who live by the sword will perish by the sword." Perhaps it was because she was a pacifist that her son—one of the great military leaders in history—is considered by the people a man of peace.

The day Ike left Kansas to go to West Point only his mother, his younger brother Milton, and his fox-terrier Flip were at home. Mrs. Eisenhower cried; Milton cried; and Flip howled.

"Milton," said Ike in a choked voice, "I'm depending on you to look after Mother." Then he grabbed his suitcase and left.

The entrance blanks young Ike filled out at the

Academy are still on file. One question was: *State if you ever wholly or partially earned your own living*. Answer: "Yes. Partially for six years and wholly for two years as refrigerating engineer. Also fireman."

Another was: *Do you use tobacco in any form?* Ike wrote, "No."

In 1911 West Point, like young Eisenhower, was coming of age. It no longer gave just technical training. Many new subjects had been added to the cadets' studies. A man who graduated from the Military Academy had a fine college education.

And West Point itself was expanding. A new gym, where Ike would make his mark as an athlete, was being built. The largest riding hall in the world was under construction. Here the boy his classmates called "Dare-devil Dwight" would demonstrate horsemanship, Kansas style.

High on the hill the great gray Cadet Chapel, dominating the West Point landscape, had recently been completed. The stained-glass windows, heavy granite arches, and colorful battle flags were an inspiration to Ike, a naturally religious boy.

Cadet Eisenhower was a good student but he received a great many demerits. He was frequently late to breakfast formation. One "quill" was for being "asleep in chair at inspection, 8:30 P.M." Another was for "Violation of orders in reference to dancing." Just what kind of dancing the future President was enjoying, the records do not say.

In the cadet slang of the day, Ike was an "area bird" (one who has to walk the area for punishment) and a "busted aristocrat" (a cadet officer who is demoted for misbehavior). He was "hivey" (quick to learn) but not a "file boner" (one who tries to beat out his classmates).

His real love was football. He was known on the gridiron as the "Kansas Cyclone." After his brilliant play during Army's attempt to defeat Jim Thorpe and the Carlisle Indians, the New York sportswriters called Ike "one of the best backs in the East."

But then bad luck struck.

When he was playing against a rugged team from Tufts College, Eisenhower hurt his knee —badly. He would never play football again. "Now," wrote a fellow cadet, "Ike must content himself with tea, tiddlywinks and talk, at all of which he excels."

As Ike lay in the cadet hospital, one thought comforted him. He had just received notice of "22 punishment tours to be served in the area *during the next 30 days*." Because of that official wording Ike had the pleasure of "walking" off his punishments while lying flat on his back!

Unwilling to give football up entirely, Ike coached the scrubs and became a varsity cheer-leader. He was leading the cheering section in November, 1914, when Army beat a much stronger Navy team by surprising it with the brand-new forward pass.

There were many famous men in Ike's class. One of his best friends was a slow-talking and fast-thinking, homespun cadet from Missouri— Omar Bradley. Ike wrote Bradley's character sketch in the *Howitzer* yearbook. What he said sounds now as though Ike could see into the future:

> "Brad's most important characteristic is 'getting there' and if he keeps up the clip he's started, some of us will some day be bragging that 'Sure, General Bradley was a classmate of mine.' "

In his first class year Ike and two classmates, Louis Merillat and Charley Benedict, formed a Woman Haters Club. They agreed not to have dates with girls or go to hops (except to get refreshments). Each put ten dollars in a pool, the entire sum to be won by the last one married. Within a year after graduation all three Woman Haters were married!

For two years Ike was appointed Cadet Color Sergeant, one of the great honors in the Corps of Cadets. He had the splendid build and the bit of dash required for proper handling of colors at official ceremonies.

The day Ike graduated, the Corps marched onto the Plain to the brisk music of "The Stars and

Stripes Forever." Immaculate and soldierly, Ike stood by the colors. At the command "Graduating class, front and center, march!" the men who were wearing the gray for the last time marched forward in a line and took their positions with the "Supe" and "Com" to review the Corps. The stirring strains of "The Dashing White Sergeant" echoed through the hills along the Hudson.

The graduation ceremony took place at Battle Monument. The tall shaft of marble gleamed in the June sunlight, a fitting memorial to the battle heroes of the Regular Army who were killed fighting for the Union in the Civil War. At nearby Trophy Point stood the heavy cannon captured in the various wars.

One hundred and sixty cadets graduated in the class of 1915, the largest class ever graduated up to that time. Ike was number 61 in academic standing. The speaker of the day was President Wilson's Secretary of War, Lindley Garrison. He might have been talking directly to Dwight D. Eisenhower when he said, "You have undertaken a great responsibility . . . Upon your conduct may depend issues of vital moment to your country."

But no one present could foresee that some day in cadet barracks there would be a small brass plaque in Ike's room, an honor few have achieved. The plaque reads:

```
┌─────────────────────────────────────────┐
│        THIS ROOM WAS OCCUPIED BY         │
│     CADET DWIGHT D. EISENHOWER           │
│        — CLASS OF 1915 —                 │
└─────────────────────────────────────────┘
```

Twenty-nine years after Ike's graduation, his serious and alert son, John, marched from cadet barracks to the West Point Field House to experience the same thrill of receiving a West Point diploma.

But Ike was absent.

The date was June 6, 1944.

On that very day, General Eisenhower, Supreme Commander of the Allied Forces, made the most crucial decision of his army career. He selected the day and hour for the greatest invasion in history. At Ike's command the huge invading ar-

mada of every type of naval craft, covered by
the mighty Allied Air Forces, was moving across
the English Channel to land on the Normandy
beaches. In the air were the daring paratroopers
ready to drop in the dark ahead of the landing.

The battle that followed was one of the great
turning points of the Second World War.

Some years later President Eisenhower returned
to West Point to attend the fortieth reunion of
his class. Before his arrival one of his aides sent
word that the President wanted to be treated
with as little formality as possible. He wanted to
be "Ike Eisenhower," not "Mister President."

During the parade of "The Old Grads" from
Cullum Hall to the statue of Colonel Thayer, the
President declined the Superintendent's invita-
tion to walk with him and the Oldest Living
Graduate at the head of the procession. The Pres-
ident insisted that he march with his class—1915.

When the parade was under way, one of his
classmates said, "Hey, Ike! Get in step!"

Ike laughed. "There's always a file boner in
every outfit."

As the Old Grads swung along to the strong

beat of "Over There," Ike stepped out of the long column to shake hands with Dick and Jimmy Walsh, cadet store tailors who had fitted Ike for his first cadet uniforms. He also hailed old Sergeant Marty Maher who, as trainer in the gym, had once "doctored" Cadet Eisenhower's injured knee.

In the gigantic new mess hall President Eisenhower addressed the members of the first class, their fathers, and two thousand graduates of other years who had gathered for a reunion. He said he had been reading a boy's book about West Point, *West Point Plebe*. In it was a story of an Old Grad who visited his former room in cadet barracks. The old-timer asked a plebe if he had ever been hazed.

"Yes, sir," the plebe replied. "I've been braced by upperclassmen. They make me stand like a ramrod."

"Humph!" snorted the Old Grad. "You don't call that *hazing*, do you? When you get to be a yearling, young man, I want you to put some teeth back into the plebe system. I think it's going to the dogs!"

Former President of the United States Dwight D. Eisenhower,
U.S.M.A. Class of 1915, presents the Eisenhower Award for
excellence in Military Psychology and Leadership to Cadet
Delbert H. Jacobs. Behind the President is the West Point Superintendent, Lieutenant General Blackshear Bryan, and the professors of the Academic Board.

Even the cadets who were about to graduate laughed at this new version of the age-old West Point joke about the Corps "going to the dogs."

At still another June Week ceremony General Eisenhower spoke to the graduating class. His remarks bore the stamp of his mother's ideas. This fighter, who is also a man of peace, said:

"After my experience I have come to hate war. It settles nothing . . . War is mankind's most tragic folly . . . to seek it is a black crime against all men. Though you follow the trade of a warrior, you do so in the spirit of Washington—not of Genghis Khan."

General Omar Bradley

BATTLE LEADERS
OF WORLD WAR II

West Point's value to the nation was never more clearly demonstrated to the public than it was during World War II.

That war was won by combined effort—by sacrifices in the homes, by men laboring in the factories and shipyards, by men serving in the air, on the sea and on the ground.

West Point did its part by supplying skilled leaders.

One of these leaders, the first man in the famous Class of 1915 to wear general's stars—as predicted by Cadet Eisenhower—was a star outfielder on the cadet baseball team and a hard-driving football halfback. His name was Omar Bradley.

The Corps of Cadets liked Bradley and when he became an officer the enlisted men liked him, too. Because of his understanding of human nature, he was called "the soldier's general." General Bradley was successful not only because of his military skills but also because of his human qualities. His kindly methods made people realize that there are many different types of effective leadership.

Bradley's and Ike's class, sometimes called "The Class the Stars Fell On," boasted more than thirty generals.

On the walls of the cadet gymnasium hang large bronze A's bearing the name of every cadet athlete who won a major sports letter. The A for the Class of 1915 shows twenty names. These twenty cadets wore a total of *thirty-two* stars as general officers in World War II.

The list of West Point men who became outstanding battle leaders in this war starts with a World War I hero—Douglas MacArthur. It includes a star athlete named Joe Stilwell, who later commanded the United States Armed Forces in China; a wrestler named Simon Bolivar Buckner, Jr., who was killed in action leading his army on Okinawa; and a varsity shortstop named Jacob Devers, who later led an army in France.

One of West Point's great leaders was General Lucius Clay who, under West Pointer General Brehon Somervell, kept the supply lines moving during World War II—an all-important task in wartime. Later it was General Clay who foiled the Russians by organizing the amazing Berlin air-lift.

Near the top of the list is the famous name of Cadet Henry "Hap" Arnold, an aviation pioneer who commanded the greatest air force ever to fly in the heavens.

One of the most colorful and dashing battle commanders was a former cadet athlete named

General Henry "Hap" Arnold

George S. Patton, Jr. In the Corps, Georgie Patton concentrated on football until he was injured, then devoted himself to the 220-yard dash and to horsemanship. The statue erected to Patton at West Point shows him in battle pose. On the base of the statue is a Patton saying: "Pursue the enemy with the utmost audacity." General Patton's armies did just that.

World War II was a global war and West Pointers made themselves felt in every part of the world. Cadet Mark Clark entered the Academy in 1913. Thirty years later he led the troops of his army to victory against the Germans in Italy. Matthew Ridgway and Maxwell Taylor parachuted with the men of their airborne divisions in the Normandy Invasion, fought in Korea, and later each became Chief of Staff of the Army.

The list of outstanding battle leaders is too long to include all the famous names in this book. The list includes not only generals, but every rank starting at second lieutenant.

There was, for example, Harry (Paddy) Flint, a good-natured cadet of Irish descent. Paddy was from Vermont. His ready wit and wide grin brought him a host of friends. He had a difficult time getting to France in World War II because authorities thought him too old to command a regiment, but Paddy Flint got there.

The men in his 39th Infantry Regiment did not think Paddy too old. They loved him. He had them stencil a peculiar device on their steel helmets: *three A's, a bar and a zero.* Colonel Flint taught his men that this was their motto; it stood for "*Anything, anywhere, anytime, bar nothing.*" And his men believed in that motto. Paddy Flint demonstrated the real "can do" spirit of a West Point battle leader until the day a sniper's bullet pierced his brain. At the time, Paddy was riding on the outside of a tank during an attack.

Bob Eichelberger, who was a first classman when Flint was a plebe, also earned a reputation as a spirited combat leader.

Cadet Eichelberger had the reputation of being a lady's man. He was prominent at the hops and had a gentle, pleasing manner. In World War II he received one of the toughest assignments given to any general.

On the New Guinea coast, the Japanese had

General George S. Patton's Monument at West Point

carved an area out of the jungle and had constructed fortifications.

The place was called Buna.

The Allies wanted Buna desperately so that they could build bases for their planes, which were needed to provide air cover for "the road" to the Philippines and Tokyo.

The Buna fortifications were guarded by the sea, the jungle, a stinking swamp, two rivers, three thousand veteran Japanese troops, and every weapon they could bring in. The Japanese were prepared to die in defense of this position if necessary.

General MacArthur sent for Eichelberger when the attack on Buna bogged down. MacArthur said, "I want you to take Buna or not come back alive."

Those orders were tough to give and tough to receive.

When Eichelberger arrived in the jungle he found many troops ill. Living conditions were terrible. There was not enough food. Almost every soldier suffered from a bad skin disease, caused by the swamp and heat, called "jungle rot." In one company every single man was running a fever. No other troops were available, so Eichelberger said, "Sick men *can* fight."

To get the demoralized men to go forward in the attack, Lieutenant General Eichelberger personally led them in hand-to-hand combat through the swamp.

As a dashing cadet, Bob Eichelberger had never dreamed of such fighting.

It was a nightmare campaign.

The enemy suffered, too. Captured Japanese diaries, translated later, told their side of the story:

> *Enemy scouts appear everywhere and attack, shooting automatic rifles. Artillery raking the area. We cannot hold out much longer.*

The United States victory at Buna was the first time in the 2,000-year history of the Japanese Empire that a Japanese fortification had been taken.

Like Flint, Eichelberger did what he asked his men to do, and like Flint he was one of West Point's victorious battle leaders.

Plebes and their dates at a square dance in the cadet gymnasium during Christmas week.

THERE'S A MONKEY
IN BARRACKS

General Matthew Ridgway, when he was Chief of Staff of the Army, wrote, "The life of a West Point cadet is brightened by many touches of humor."

Cadet humor dates back to the beginning of West Point. Each period has had its own particular brand of fun; at no time have the cadets been too busy to amuse themselves. They are aided by the unwritten rule that an officer must *catch* the cadet playing a prank; he cannot ask, "Who did it?"

A hundred years ago there was an unpopular tactical officer named Lieutenant Thomas Wilton. The cadets called him "The Prize Baby," "The Mammoth Pig" and "The Fatted Calf," and they did their best to make life miserable for him. To impress some ladies, Lieutenant Wilton once sent a plebe to the guard room to ask for the parole and countersign—the passwords for the night. The messenger came back with a paper which read:

Parole . . . . Fatted
Countersign . . . . Calf

The tactical officer did not think it was funny.

In the middle '80s, excess energy was often worked off in summer camp by a stag dance in one of the company streets, the area between two rows of tents. Muskets, with bayonets fixed, were stacked in a tripod and a candle was placed on the end of each bayonet. Cadets with violins and drums formed the orchestra.

The dance got faster and faster, the dancers attempting to keep up with the music. It was a weird form of endurance contest. The winner was the one who moved his hands and feet the fastest and was still in action at the finish.

After World War I the "runts" and "flankers" (short and tall cadets) played a football game every Thanksgiving. After the game, the excited cadets staged water battles which almost wrecked the barracks.

The officers put a stop to this.

The annual Thanksgiving game then became a contest between the "goats" and "engineers" of the junior class. ("Goats" are cadets poorest in their studies; "engineers" are those at the top of the class.) In this game the numbers on the players' backs correspond to the cadets' class standing. On the same field you can see No. 1 and No. 590.

One of the best-loved cadets to enter West Point was Maurice F. Daly, of Hartford, Connecticut. "Moe" Daly was a star center on the football team and a fine hockey and lacrosse player. He had a ready Irish wit and a broad grin, and he liked practical jokes.

In the mess hall, when the Officer in Charge was not looking, Daly would sometimes throw a baked potato as far as he could. And Daly had a good arm!

The whole Corps enjoyed Daly's sense of humor. One rainy Saturday at inspection the tactical officer, Major "Jake" Bagby, lifted the cape of Moe Daly's raincoat and said to a nearby cadet officer, "Report Mister Daly for cutting the sleeves out of his raincoat." This was a lapse of memory on Bagby's part, for cadets' raincoats have no sleeves.

Daly and the cadets within earshot did not smile, although they thought this a great joke. The next day the report was posted: *"Daly, M. F. —cutting sleeves out of raincoat."*

It was Daly's privilege to explain the report, but he would not do it. He waited to see how many demerits Bagby would give him. He received three. Daly never protested. He said, "It's worth three demerits to have a laugh on an officer."

Moe Daly liked to get a waiter in the mess hall to change coats with him. He would "wrestle" with the waiter and pretend to throw him under the table. Under the table, the waiter would put on Daly's gray dress coat and would then sit in Daly's chair. Cadet Daly, in the waiter's white jacket, would arise, grab an empty dish and head for the kitchen. The cadets laughed uproariously whenever Moe did this. It took skillful maneuvering on Daly's part to avoid the Officer in Charge.

Moe never missed a chance to play a prank. Once the Chief Magistrate of the City of New York, Judge Edgar Bromberger, gave a dinner party for the football squad and their dates at the Astor Hotel after an Army-Navy game. Daly, and another cadet at the football training table named Reeder, decided to take a waiter from the cadet mess to the judge's party as a "distinguished guest."

These two cadets spent many days prior to the dinner giving the untutored waiter lessons in table manners and introductions.

On the night of the party Daly and Reeder dressed the waiter in a tuxedo borrowed from Cadet Skinner. They placed a broad red ribbon across the waiter's stiff white shirt front and escorted him to the party.

After greeting his host Cadet Daly said, "Judge Bromberger, may I present our friend, Count Mepopolis of Greece?"

The waiter bowed from the waist as he had been taught to do.

Judge Bromberger smiled and said, "I am honored, sir."

During dinner the football squad chuckled secretly as they watched the waiter play the part of the count.

It was not until the end of the evening that the joke was discovered. Reeder's father, who was also a guest, realized the nobleman was a fraud when he heard "the Count from Greece" criticize the manner in which the Astor Hotel waiters were serving the cadets!

Like young men at any college, cadets find ways of amusing themselves despite the rules.

There is the matter of pets, for example. West Point regulations state: "There will be no pets in barracks." This has always been a challenge. There have been monkeys in barracks, hidden in specially built trunk-lockers. There have been hamsters and white mice concealed in laundry bags and shoe boxes. Goldfish have swum contentedly in cadets' water buckets. Parakeets have been hidden in the chimneys.

Cadets have had gardens in the area of barracks and TV sets cleverly concealed in trunk rooms. There have been popcorn machines and hot plates on which cadets have prepared hamburgers for sale to other cadets—all without the knowledge of the Tacs.

West Point has had many extraordinary tactical officers, but Lieutenant Colonel Edward McConnell was one of the most unusual. McConnell was bald and had a large, hooked nose. He also had a sense of humor. The cadets called him "The Owl."

One night the Owl was inspecting at Camp Buckner, the summer training camp six miles west of West Point. A cadet sentinel heard a strange

noise. He flashed a light in the face of the inspecting officer and gasped, "Holy Smoke! It's the
Owl!"

The Owl hooted, "Who-o-o-o-o-o! Let me
pass."

Once when the Owl was on duty as Officer in
Charge in the mess hall, he saw Cadet Mike Lion
moving from table to table in search of extra milk.
Cadets are supposed to keep their seats during a
meal, so the Owl wrote up the report:

"Lion roaming around mess hall."

Another tactical officer with a sense of humor
was Captain "Pop" Goode. Pop, a big burly fellow,
knew most of the tricks because he had been a
mischievous cadet himself.

Once, when inspecting uniforms, Pop ordered a
cadet to get rid of a worn-out pair of trousers. Pop
noted the look of disappointment on the cadet's
face.

Pop's next inspection of cadet rooms took place
when the cadets were in class. He searched par-
ticularly for the worn-out pair of trousers and
found them in the cadet's laundry bag. Pop gave
the cadet two demerits.

The next day Pop discovered the trousers hidden under the mattress. This time the cadet received ten demerits. Deciding that the trousers were piling up more demerits for him than they were worth, the cadet got rid of them.

But Pop Goode was a man who made sure. And when the cadet returned from class on the third day he found his room turned upside down! Clothing had been pulled out of his locker, his bed torn apart and his laundry bag emptied.

On the table was a note from Pop: "I give up. Where are they?"

Colonel Red Blaik, the famous football coach, also has a sense of humor. Once he took his coaching staff out into the hills back of West Point where the plebes were on a practice hike. Blaik was concerned because he thought the cadets were not enjoying themselves as they had "in the old days." He asked a friend who had been a cadet prankster to talk about mischievous pranks of the past. The coach wanted to give the cadets some ideas on how to amuse themselves.

While Blaik's friend was talking about jokes cadets had played in bygone days, upperclassmen just out of earshot undressed a plebe sentinel and left him walking post without his clothes!

There have been many, many jokes by cadets. They have ranged all the way from putting the baseball coach on guard dressed in cadet clothing, to painting BEAT NAVY on the sides of a destroyer anchored in the Hudson. Cadets have even "stolen" the Navy goat before an Army-Navy football game.

Like Ben Franklin, West Point cadets understand the value of laughter.

A platoon of cadets passing in review

A BATTLE LEADER
OF KOREA

On a cold wintry day in 1949 a crowd gathered in the West Point field house near the finish line of the track. Around the turn came a group of runners on their fourth lap of the mile. The starter fired his pistol, signaling that this was the last lap of the race. The yells of cadets and officers

179

mingled with the cries of visiting spectators as the runners tore by. A sturdy athlete was seen to pull out of the pack and forge ahead.

A professor, acting as timer, looked at his stop watch and smiled.

"The boy's making fine time," he said. "He's going to win. He's going to be one of our best distance men."

As the milers increased their speed, the judges took their position at the tape.

"Come on, Shea!" screamed the plebes. "Come on, Dick!"

The yells echoed in the girders of the huge building as the runners came down the home stretch to the finish line. In a minute the loudspeaker boomed: "New plebe indoor record for the mile run—by Cadet Shea. Time: 4 minutes 26.5 seconds."

The professor's remark proved correct, for the five-foot nine-inch, 160-pound cadet broke record after record in the mile and two-mile runs. Each fall he raced over the cross-country course in the hills in back of Michie Stadium. He soon established himself as a cross-country champion.

The Corps liked Shea. Not only was he a winner, but he was modest and quiet as well, with a ready smile. He developed a reputation for being able to do any task given him efficiently and faithfully. The letter men on the squad elected him captain of the track team. The Tactical Department awarded him the chevrons of a cadet captain.

In his three years on the varsity, Shea won nine championship races and set five Academy track records. He was the cross-country champion in the IC4-A, which is the abbreviation for Intercollegiate Amateur Athletic Association of America. Shea was crowned Heptagonal champion in distance runs for three straight years, something no other runner has ever accomplished.

When the gun barked for Shea's last race in May, 1952, the Navy's best miler challenged him. But Shea was not in that race to lose. On the third lap he pulled ahead and flashed across the finish line to win, equaling his own record set in a previous Army-Navy track meet.

The next few days were busy ones for Dick. At a parade of the Corps, he accepted the Army Athletic Association trophy awarded to the outstanding athlete in the graduating class. He received his diploma from the Superintendent, then led his bride, Joyce Riemann, through the traditional arch of sabers at the church.

And then new Lieutenant Shea faced a hard decision. Should he compete in the Olympic Games or should he continue his military training?

Shea felt it was his *duty* to make himself into a well-trained leader. So he gave up the Olympics and took his bride to Fort Benning, Georgia, where he attended the Infantry School.

When the Communists invaded South Korea, Lieutenant Shea sailed for the Far East with other members of his class.

One night, thirteen months after his graduation at West Point, First Lieutenant Shea inspected the battle lines his company was holding on Porkchop Hill. All was quiet. He saw that the soldiers of his company, "A" of the 17th Infantry Reg-

Cadet Dick Shea, U.S.M.A. Class of 1952, leading on the left, wins the 1 mile race in 4 minutes, 13.4 seconds, establishing a new record at the Heptagonal Games Association 18th Annual Outdoor Championships at West Point.

iment, were ready. He was second-in-command of the unit.

Suddenly the roar of light machine guns, automatic rifles and M-1's cut through the night. Red flashes in the darkness outlined the company's position. Flares were shot up to illuminate the enemy. Messages were sent to the mortars and artillery—"The enemy is attacking in force."

The noise and confusion were terrific.

On his own, Lieutenant Shea got together men of his company and led a counterattack against the hordes of Communist troops. In hand-to-hand fighting, he killed two enemy soldiers with a trench knife.

All night long the company's position was in peril. And at dawn the enemy tried harder to overrun Porkchop Hill. Men from another company joined Shea's company. He felt it was his *duty* to charge the enemy and he did so.

In this attack he was wounded but refused to go to the rear. He did not want to leave his men. Despite the wound he led a group against an enemy machine gun, killing three more enemy soldiers by firing his carbine and by throwing grenades.

He worked through the next night to reorganize the company. At daybreak, back came the Communists. Shea led the counterattack again and was last seen in fierce hand-to-hand combat.

Captain Roberts, commanding the company, reported Dick missing in action and said, "I have never seen such courage displayed by any man."

Two years later the Secretary of the Army, acting in the name of President Eisenhower and the Congress of the United States, pinned The Medal of Honor, our country's highest award, on Dick's twenty-month-old son.

Major General "Skippy" Harbold, himself a famous West Point athlete, and the commander of the Eastern Air Defense Force, said about Dick Shea: "The lieutenants—our first line leaders—are vitally important men in combat, regardless of the branch of service. When our Country has men like Dick Shea, the mission of West Point is accomplished."

Many other Americans have expressed pride in our Military Academy. It is one of the great institutions of the world. As long as our Country has West Point it can count on the kind of leadership that wins in war as well as peace.

INDEX